1

2

25. NOV

28. APR

3

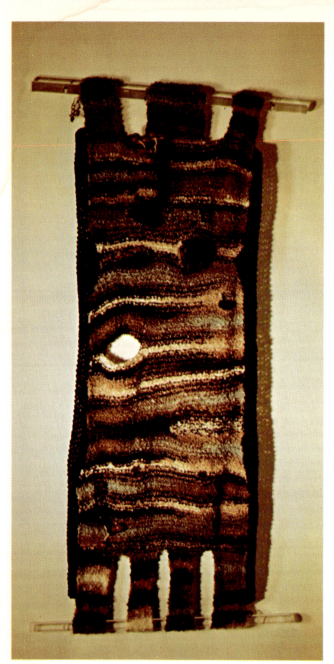

4

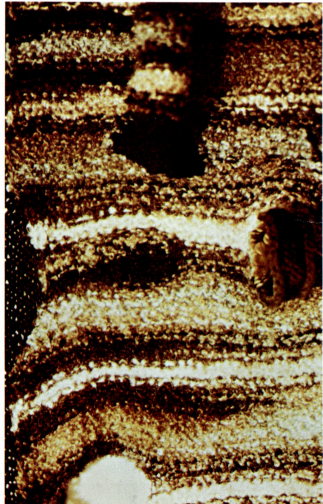

5

6

7

8

9

10

12

11

13

14

15

19

18

16

17

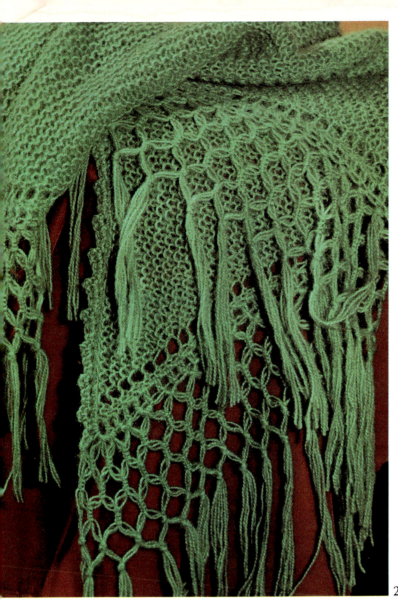

20

21

22

23

24

25

KNIT ART

Ferne Geller Cone

VNR **VAN NOSTRAND REINHOLD COMPANY**

NEW YORK　CINCINNATI　TORONTO　LONDON　MELBOURNE

746.432

Van Nostrand Reinhold Company
New York   Cincinnati   Toronto   London   Melbourne

Van Nostrand Reinhold Company Regional Offices:
New York   Cincinnati   Chicago   Millbrae   Dallas
Van Nostrand Reinhold Company International Offices:
London   Toronto   Melbourne

Copyright © 1975 by Litton Educational Publishing, Inc.
Library of Congress Catalog Card Number 74–16736
ISBN 0–442–21655–6 (cloth)
       0–442–21656–4 (paper)

Designed by Loudan Enterprises

Published by Van Nostrand Reinhold Company
A Division of Litton Educational Publishing, Inc.
450 West 33rd Street, New York, N.Y. 10001
16 15 14 13 12 11 10 9 8 7 6 5 4 3 2 1

Library of Congress Cataloging in Publication Data
Cone, Ferne Geller.
   Knit art.
   Bibliography; p.
   Includes index.
   1. Knitting.   2. Soft sculpture.   I. Title.
TT820.C783   746.4'3   74-16736
ISBN 0-442-21655-6
ISBN 0-442-21656-4 pbk.

C-1. An array of tools and yarns. (Photograph by Roy Goodall)

C-2. Circular needles, handmade with plastic cable and wooden doweling. (Photograph by Roy Goodall)

C-3. *Columns*. Hanging, knitted in wool and mohair and trimmed with wooden beads. Stockinette and garter stitch with size 11 needles. 72″ long x 24″ wide. (Photograph by Roy Goodall)

C-4 and C-5. *Variegated*. Hanging, knitted in a wool-and-mohair blend. Stockinette stitch with size 9 needles. 30″ long x 18″ wide. (Photographs by Roy Goodall)

C-6. *Venturi*. Hanging, knitted in linen slub and thick-and-thin gold rayon. Stockinette stitch on sizes 9, 11, and 13 circular needles. 48″ long x 24″ wide. (Photograph by Roy Goodall)

C-7. Hanging, knitted in handspun wool. Circular knitting and ribbon stitch. Knitted by a student of Rosalie King, University of Washington. (Photograph by Mary Jane Anderson)

C-8. *My Cup Runneth Over, and Over, and Over . . . .* Sculpture in jute, knitted, crocheted, and trimmed with overlay. Garter stitch and single and double crochet stitch on size 15 circular needles and a size K crochet hook. Stuffed with shredded foam. (Photograph by Ray Kaltenbach)

C-9. *Olympiad*. Hanging, knitted and crocheted in sisal, horsehair, and handspun wool and stretched on an armature of four wrapped hula hoops. Stockinette stitch on size 35 needles and single, double, and filet crochet stitch with a size K hook. (Photograph by Scotty Sapiro)

C-10. *Clem*. Knitted in the round in German wool and jute with plastic cable. (Photograph by Roy Goodall)

C-11. *Naturals II*. Hanging, knitted and crocheted in white leather lacing and handspun, vegetable-dyed wool. Wrap stitch and single crochet. 48″ long x 16″ wide. (Collection of Gladys Nelson; photograph by Roy Goodall)

C-12. *Mexicana*. Collar, crocheted in fake suede and trimmed with shells, lava-rock beads, bones, and wooden beads. Single crochet. (Photograph by Mary Jane Anderson)

C-13. *Puff 'n Stuff*. Hanging, knitted in fake suede and jute and stuffed. Stockinette stitch, garter stitch, and double knitting on size 10 needles. 108″ long x 24″ wide. (Photograph by Roy Goodall)

C-14. Hanging, made in jute and trimmed with beads. Knitted by a student of Rosalie King, University of Washington. (Photograph by Mary Jane Anderson)

C-15. *Grommets*. Hanging, knitted in seine twine and trimmed with grommets. Wrap stitch and stockinette stitch on size 17 needles. 48″ long x 30″ wide. (Collection of Joan Hammer; photograph by Roy Goodall)

C-16. Hanging, made in blue wool and trimmed with wooden beads and brass bells. Knitted by a student of Rosalie King, University of Washington. (Photograph by Mary Jane Anderson)

C-17. Detail of *Owl* (see Figure 10-4). (Photograph by Mike Sedam)

C-18. Hanging, made in handspun wool, stuffed with unspun wool, trimmed with bells, and hung from old garden shears. Knitted by Susan Ogilvie, a workshop student of the author. (Photograph by Susan Ogilvie)

C-19. *Owgle*. Hanging, knitted in natural linen and recycled wool and trimmed with wooden beads. 18″ long x 12″ wide. (Photograph by Roy Goodall)

C-20. Shawl, knitted, crocheted, and macraméd in mohair. Made by Anne Hawkins. (Photograph by Mary Jane Anderson)

C-21. Loincloth, crocheted in double-strand gold brocade. Single, double, and pineapple crochet stitch. (Modeled by Ruth Cowan; photograph by Roy Goodall)

C-22 and C-23. Man's caftan, knitted and crocheted in knitting worsted. Stockinette stitch and double crochet stitch. (Photographs by Roy Goodall)

C-24. *Celia's Jools*. Sculpture, crocheted and knitted in plastic twine, black and brown lamé, and gold, silver, and charcoal brocade and stuffed with plastic bags. Single and double crochet stitch and stockinette stitch. 70″ long. (Photograph by Roy Goodall)

C-25. *Nefertiti's Girdle*. Belt, crocheted in bronze brocade. Single crochet. (Photograph by Mary Jane Anderson)

Frontispiece. Detail of *Hawaii* (see Figure 8-2). (Photograph by Roy Goodall)

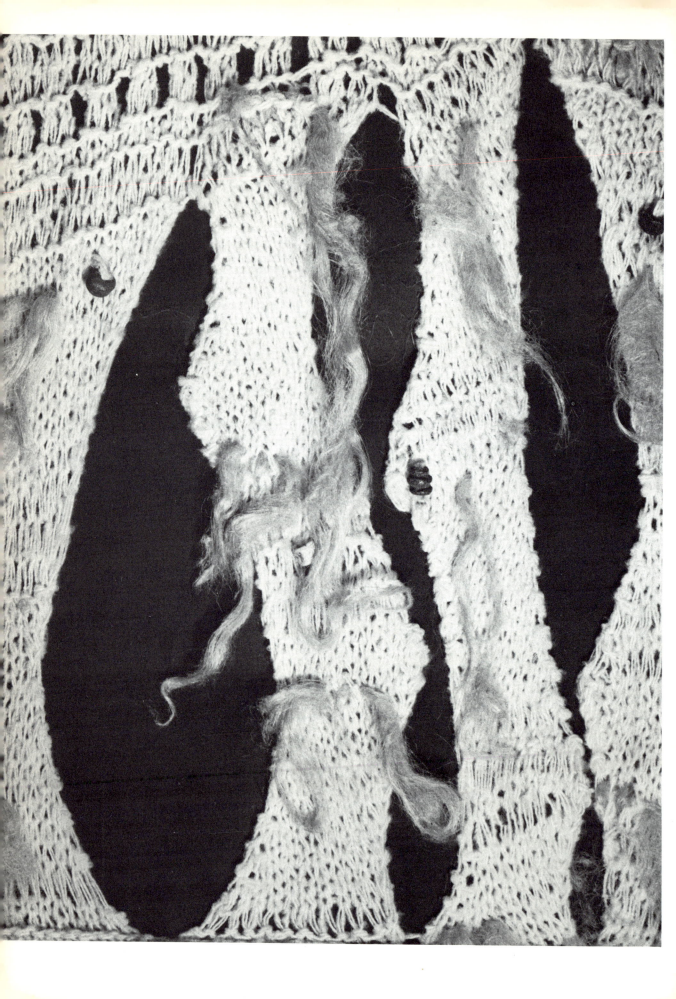

CONTENTS

Acknowledgments   14

Introduction   15

1. Get Ready   17

2. Shape It   21

3. Color It   36

4. Materials Matter   40

5. You're In Stitches   48

6. Feel It   57

7. Look Around You   61

8. Buttons and Beads   65

9. Tie It All Up   69

10. Hang It All   76

11. Fashion-Wise   82

12. Simple Crochet   88

Bibliography   101

Suppliers   102

Index   103

ACKNOWLEDGMENTS

My sincere thanks to my friend Jean Wilson, who so generously shared her expertise, both as a craftswoman and as an author; to Nancy Newman at Van Nostrand Reinhold, who thought my approach to knitting should be shared; to Jane Thompson and Mabel Knoertzer, whose nimble fingers knitted many of the experimental pieces; to the teachers and students who were such willing guinea pigs; to Mary Jane Anderson, Roy Goodall, and Mike Sedam, photographers; to Rachel Osterlof, for her painstaking line drawings; to Wendy Lochner, for editing the manuscript; and to the artists who allowed me to include examples of their work.

Many thanks also to Mary Scott, for her help in coordinating the photographs and for her expert indexing; to my daughter Wendy and my friends Ruth Cowan and Leonard Frye, for their patient modeling; to the American Crafts Council, for supplying valuable information; to my daughter Carol, for her assistance in proofreading the manuscript; and especially to Gladys Nelson, who, in addition to reading the manuscript with an expert's eye and steering me in the right direction, thoroughly understood and approved of what I wanted to say.

And most of all to my husband, Morton, who encouraged me from the beginning and was always there when I needed him.

INTRODUCTION

Knitting is a marvelously flexible craft. It is also a much maligned one. Why this contradiction? Is it because pattern stitches are so complicated that many people give up hope and hide their attempts in a drawer, vowing never to try again? Or is it even more because the results seem so limited — sweaters, socks, booties, afghans, all knit to rigid pattern instructions that allow no freedom to create?

The purpose of this book is to present an alternative approach to traditional knitting: knitting as an art form rather than merely a utilitarian craft; knitting to be looked at and admired for itself, not simply to be put to functional uses. And a sense of accomplishment and enjoyment should accompany every stitch — half the fun should be in the doing.

Knit art has grown naturally out of my own knitting and design experience. Until recently, I was a designer of handknit garments. I employed what was then a practically unknown approach: to handle handknit fabric exactly like woven fabric — to cut and sew it in order to achieve a couturier finish and to emphasize the physical design of the garment rather than the pattern of the material. Frankly, pattern stitches, except in unusual instances, left me cold. Like a print dress worn several days in a row, they were often very tiring and very dated. Because so many hours of work went into each garment, I wanted my knits to be worn and enjoyed for years.

Careful assembling and finishing became my personal code, but I was not averse to using any shortcuts that could be devised to speed up the process. Those years instilled in me an appreciation of fibers and of simplicity in design.

In 1963, I started a yarn shop in order to share this point of view on handknit fashions. I offered it as an alternative to the standard methods taught in other yarn shops in the area. Its immediate acceptance was gratifying.

Just two years ago, the Henry Gallery at the University of Washington invited me to conduct a workshop in Imaginative Knitting. I was not quite sure what that meant, so I began to experiment with shapes and forms, drawing from all the fashion-design techniques I'd accumulated over the years, but exaggerating and simplifying them, creating spontaneously as I knitted. From this evolved my conception of *knit art*.

I determined to find out if knit art was for everyone; workshops and lectures with different age groups in schools, galleries, and retirement homes demonstrated that almost everyone can learn the techniques and have fun.

Several of my students in Rosalie King's Fiber Analysis class at the University of Washington had never held a pair of knitting needles before, but they became so intrigued by the artistic prospects of this free-form approach that they taught themselves the basics so that they could participate. With this minimal knowledge, the same students produced many imaginative pieces, some of which are shown throughout the book. I'm convinced that this was largely due to the fact that they had never learned constrictive rules to begin with, so they were totally original in their designs.

It was exhilarating to observe the positive reactions of workshop students — their relief at not having to follow intricate patterns and their pleasure in discovering new, artistic possibilities in knitting. Their excitement was high, and I hope that your response will be the same. Let your fingers fly, creating intoxicating yarnscapes of whatever strikes your fancy!

I-1. Students at the author's workshop in Seattle, Washington.

1.

GET READY

Spontaneous knitting is the theme of this book. Your efforts will be that much more enjoyable if you have the right tools on hand and are familiar with the standard terms and abbreviations (knitting patterns are always abbreviated).

TOOLS AND MATERIALS

In conventional knitting, it is important to have the exact needle size for a specific gauge (the number of stitches per inch), and a tape measure is an absolute necessity. Here, you can forget about gauges, and you can hide your tape measure — you won't need it. You will need different sizes of needles, however, to give more scope to your creative efforts. You should also have a crochet hook or two (to pick up dropped stitches or to weave in loose ends), some stitch markers (you can buy plastic markers at yarn shops and sewing centers, but colored yarn will do), a blunt-pointed yarn needle with a big eye, a box of T-pins, and a pair of scissors.

Let's begin with the needles. Knitting needles can be straight or circular, and they come in a variety of sizes and materials (see Figure C-1). The straight needles range in size from 00 to 50 (on an increasing scale in the United States but on a decreasing scale in England) and in length from seven to ten to fourteen inches. The length you use depends upon the size of your project. I use a ten-inch needle whenever I can; it is easier to handle, and it doesn't interfere with my movements. Straight knitting needles used to be made from steel, bone, silver, ivory, and even iron, but now they are usually plastic, aluminum, or wood. All are acceptable.

Wooden needles are available in sizes 15 and 17, or you can make your own from wooden doweling (see Figure 1-1). Hardware and lumber stores sell doweling in many sizes. Sand handmade needles carefully with very fine, moistened steel wool, and apply two coats of a clear, plastic finish (Varathane is excellent) so that the stiches will slide freely on the shaft. All wooden needles should be sanded down and refinished occasionally in any case, since they may become rough from abrasive fibers such as jute, coarse linen, or sisal.

Since I often flit from one project to another, I find it expedient to have many different kinds and sizes of needles on hand. The aluminum needles are my favorites — the surface stays smooth, and the points are more definite — but unfortunately, size 19 seems to be the largest available.

Plastic needles are lighter in weight, but they break more easily. Another disadvantage is that the warmth of your hands tends to cause synthetic yarns to adhere to the needles, making it harder to slide the stitches.

A set or two of double-pointed needles is a good investment. These come four to a set in sizes 00 to 15, and, although you may not use them as often, they are convenient for working smaller areas in the round.

Circular needles are available in sizes 0 to 15, and they come in several lengths, from six inches to thirty-six inches. In addition to knitting in the round, they may also be used instead of straight needles for knitting back and forth. They are sometimes preferable for work that requires an extraordinarily large number of stitches. A kit of interchangeable circular-needle

1-1. Needles made from wooden doweling. (Photograph by Mary Jane Anderson)

parts is worth obtaining; it allows you to change both the size and the length of the needle in the middle of your work without disturbing the fabric. You can also make your own circular needles from lengths of plastic or rubber hose and doweling (see Figure C-2). The doweling points must fit firmly into the hose, or they will come loose while you are working. If you fasten the doweling to the hose with clear, plastic glue, the needle will be strong enough to accommodate the weight of the material.

In addition to knitting needles, a crochet hook is a very useful tool — for weaving in loose threads; for picking up dropped stitches; for adding a border. They are inexpensive, so you can have several sizes for different thicknesses of yarns and fibers. They, too, are available in many materials — aluminum, steel, plastic, and wood. Aluminum hooks are about six inches long and are sized by letter from A (smallest) through K (largest). They are especially practical for traditional knitting yarns and cords. Steel hooks are only available in smaller sizes and are sized by number — 14 (finest) to 00 (largest). They are recommended for fine linen, cotton, and other lightweight yarns. Wooden hooks are sized from 10 (smallest) to 16 (largest). These are quite large and are great for very bulky yarns and fibers or several strands of yarns used together. Like wooden needles, they should be treated to a couple of coats of the clear, liquid plastic. For extremely thick, heavy ropes, monster-size plastic hooks are available.

I prefer T-pins to the ordinary dressmaker pins. They are stronger and more practical for heavier fibers. The double crossbar at the top will keep the fabric from slipping off, and they make a firm anchor when you steam your fabric.

The blunt-pointed yarn needle with a big eye will prevent yarn from splitting, and the big eye will hold several strands of yarn.

Markers are rings of plastic that are sized to fit knitting needles up to 15. They are useful for keeping track of patterns in your work or for reminding you when to change needles. Colored-yarn markers are more practical when you are using the larger needles.

Unlike traditional knitting, you'll be working with a greater variety of fibers and yarns, so you should familiarize yourself with what is available. Natural fibers include cotton, wool, silk, jute, raffia, flax, sisal, and even paper, and all of these can be found in many different weights and thicknesses. Experiment to find the ones you most enjoy working with.

Man-made fibers are plastic, nylon, Orlon, fiberglass, rayon, and many others too numerous to mention here.

There are also synthetic- and natural-fiber blends such as nylon and cotton or wool, wool and rayon, and dozens of other combinations. All of these come in many weights and thicknesses too.

In addition, check out the novelty yarns such as straw, metallic, and ribbion.

Slub yarns have thick sections that are less twisted, which when knitted give an uneven, raised texture to your fabric.

With the great variety of weights, thicknesses, and colors of both natural and synthetic yarns and fibers, you'll have no trouble finding materials to work with. What is important is how you put them together.

BASIC KNITTING TERMS

Knit art does not require absolute precision, so needle sizes and complicated patterns are not as important as they are in traditional knitting. However, as with any craft, the more you know, the more satisfaction you will derive from your efforts. If you've never knitted, you should familiarize yourself with the following basic terms and standard abbreviations so that you will be able to follow a printed pattern:

K	Knit: to insert the needle into the front of the stitch and bring the yarn under and over the needle.
P	Purl: with yarn in front, to insert the needle from back to front of the stitch and bring yarn over and under the needle.
Lp	Loop: the rounded fold of yarn that is the basis of every kind of stitch in knitting.
B	Back: to work in the back loop of a stitch.
K1b	Knit one stitch through back loop of stitch.
P1b	Purl one stitch through back loop of stitch.
St(es)	Stitch(es).
Sl st	Slip stitch: to slip a stitch from one needle to the other.
Tog	Together: to work two stitches together.
K2 tog	Knit two stitches together.
P2 tog	Purl two stitches together.
Sl stpw	Slip a stitch from one needle to another purlwise.
Inc	Increase: to knit into the front and back of the same stitch to make two stitches.
Dec	Decrease: to knit or purl two stitches together to make one stitch out of two.
Yo	Yarn over: to wrap the yarn around the needle to make a new stitch.
Psso	Pass slip stitch over: to pass one stitch over another stitch.
Beg	Beginning.
Pat	Pattern.
Pat st	Pattern stitch: a group of stitches over one or more rows, which are repeated to form a pattern; the steps are enclosed by asterisks (* . . . *).
St st	Stockinette stitch: to alternate a row of knitting and a row of purling.
G st	Garter stitch: to knit every row.
Mc	Main color.
Cc	Contrasting color.
Rnd	Round: circular knitting.
Dpn	Double-pointed needle.
In(es)	Inch(es).
Rem	Remaining.
Rep	Repeat.
Co	Cast on: to put the first set of stitches on the needle.
Bo	Bind off: to form an edge by slipping the first of two stitches over the second and repeating across the row.
Ksb	Knit into stitch below: to knit into a stitch in the row below the one that is being worked, dropping the stitch in the latter.

2.
SHAPE IT

It's amazing how many shapes you can create with your knitting needles. You can make huge, bulky, mountainous shapes; tiny, lacy, fragile shapes; shapes that have rhythm; and shapes that are as plain and starkly beautiful as the earth's flatlands. There are diamonds, triangles, trees, mushrooms, rectangles, squares, holes, and slits — all simple to make and fun to develop. This chapter will show you how to knit lots of shapes. How you use them is up to you.

It's a good idea to make an experimental piece of each of the shapes described in this chapter; it will come in handy for reference when you're looking for a special design. You can use either garter stitch or stockinette stitch, but after finishing each pattern or shape, always go back to the original number of stitches. Work several rows of garter stitch between each of your experiments to separate them, and label the methods and needle sizes in each instance.

CHANGING SHAPE BY CHANGING NEEDLES

For your experimental piece, you will need a skein of knitting worsted or another yarn of similar weight and a variety of needles ranging, for example, from sizes 8 through 35. You may use whatever needles you have on hand, but do include a few larger ones.

Cast twenty stitches onto a size 8 needle, and work several rows in garter stitch. Now, knit a few more rows of garter stitch with a size 19 needle, then with a size 35 needle. You will soon discover that your work becomes lacier and wider with successively larger needles (see Figure 2-1). Now work the foregoing sequence in reverse — a lacy, oval pattern is created without varying the number of stitches in a row just by using different sizes of needles in sequence.

2-1.

INCREASING AND DECREASING

2-2.

RIBBONS

On the same practice piece, you can create many kinds of shapes with only one size needle by increasing and decreasing the number of stitches in a row. In other words, by adding stitches, your work will become wider, and conversely, when you subtract stitches, it will become narrower.

Work one row of twenty stitches, then, on the next row, increase one stitch in each stitch all the way across the row. (You should now have forty stitches on the needle.) Purl back. Work even on these forty stitches for two or three inches, ending with a purl row. On the next row, knit the first two stitches together, and continue decreasing in this manner across the row. Purl back. The increasing and decreasing produces a ripple or ribbon effect. Try this technique with different sizes of needles, working a few rows of garter stitch between each needle change so you can see and feel the difference in texture. The ribbons in Figure 2-2 were made with sizes 35, 19, and 8 needles, respectively.

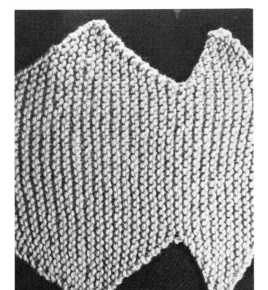

2-3.

DIAMONDS AND TRIANGLES

You can also change the shape of your work by increasing and decreasing at the beginning and the end of a row. For example, assuming that you still have twenty stitches on the needle and that you are working in garter stitch, *increase* one stitch at the beginning and the end of every other row ten times, then *decrease* at each end of every other row until you are back to the original twenty stitches (Figure 2-3). This creates a diamond shape (Figure 2-4).

To exaggerate the shape, increase one stitch at the beginning and end of *every* row instead of every other row ten times (Figure 2-5), then decrease *every* row ten times.

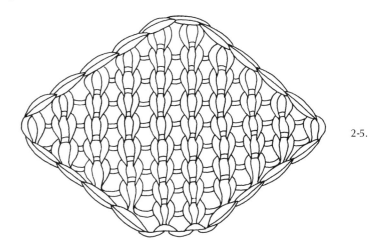

2-5.

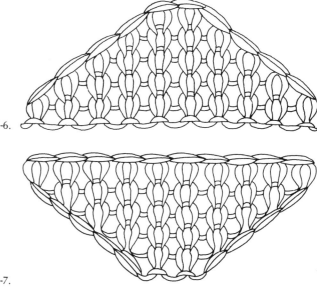

2-4.

To make a triangle, start with a larger number of stitches, (forty stitches, for example), decrease one stitch on each side of every other row until two stitches remain on the needle, then reverse the procedure (Figure 2-6). This is the opposite of the diamond pattern. Or you can make an inverted triangle by starting with only two stitches and increasing at the beginning and end of every other row (Figure 2-7). Try this technique with different sizes of needles to see the variety of patterns that can be achieved simply by increasing and decreasing.

2-6.

2-7.

SHORT ROWS

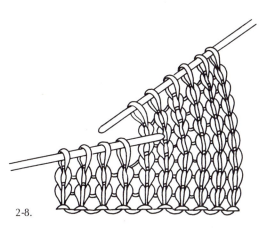

2-8.

2-9.

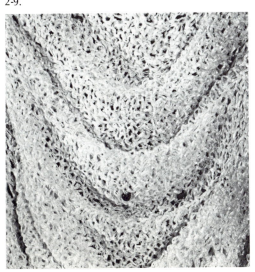

Curves are among the most graceful and versatile shapes. You can make them by knitting *short rows*. This technique is often used to shape the tops of knitted skirts or the shoulders of sweaters, but it is easily adapted to knit art.

On your practice piece, working in stockinette stitch with twenty stitches on your needle, knit across ten stitches. Turn and purl back. On the next row, work across twelve stitches, turn, and purl back. Continue in this mannner, working two more stitches on the left-hand needle (see Figure 2-8). Purl back. On the next row, knit all the way across.

This method produces a curve on one side only (Figure 2-9), but you can make a curve on the opposite side simply by reversing the procedure. By working both sides simultaneously, you can achieve a two-way curve. Here's how: knit across until eight stitches remain on the left-hand needle. Turn your work, and purl across until eight stitches remain on the left-hand needle. Turn again, and knit until six stitches remain on the left-hand needle. Continue working and turning until there are only four stitches remaining on the needle, then knit all the way across to complete the short-row sequence. This sequence does not *require* a two-stitch interval on each turn. You may want a sharper curve — turn after only one stitch — or perhaps a more gentle one — turn after knitting three more stitches. Try your own variations. What kind of yarn and what needle size you use will determine to a large extent how you adapt the short rows. Play around a bit — experimenting is half the fun.

To create a piece with several more pronounced drapes, repeat this pattern, but between each curve knit or purl two stitches together across one row, then knit or purl back across another row, increasing one stitch in every stitch.

Figures 2-10 and 2-11 show a lovely drapery effect achieved with this method of short rows. It was knitted on size 19 needles in a basic garter stitch. The texture of the yarn and the shape of the hanging add to the visual interest.

The short-row method of draping is not recommended for relatively inflexible fibers such as leather lacing or jute; they are too rigid to fall well. Cotton, linen, wool, and some synthetics and blends are better suited to this technique. Here again, you'll never know the possibilities of a fiber unless you give it a try.

2-10 and 2-11. *Softly, Softly*. Hanging, knitted in opaque white plastic twine and cotton slub yarn and trimmed with multicolored wooden beads. 65" long x 30" wide. (Photograph by Mike Sedam)

CASTING ON AND BINDING OFF

Another way to create interesting shapes is by casting on and binding off stitches at various points throughout your project.

The *Greek key* is one effect that can be achieved with this technique. Again, begin with twenty stitches, and work two or three inches of garter stitch. At the beginning of the next row, cast on ten stitches. (Cast on in the usual manner, but instead of leaving the first loop on the right-hand needle, slip the worked stitch back to the left-hand needle. Slip the right-hand needle into the loop you have just knitted, knit another stitch, and place this stitch on the left-hand needle. Continue in this way until you have ten loops on the needle.) Knit across the row, turn, and cast on ten stitches at the beginning of the next row. Work back and forth in garter stitch for as many rows as you need. When these are completed, bind off ten stitches at the beginning of the next row, and work across the remaining stitches. Bind off ten more stitches at the beginning of the following row, and work across the row to return to the original twenty stitches. Knit as many rows of garter stitch as you did in the previous sequence, then cast on again as before. Continue the entire procedure until the desired length is reached (see Figure 2-12).

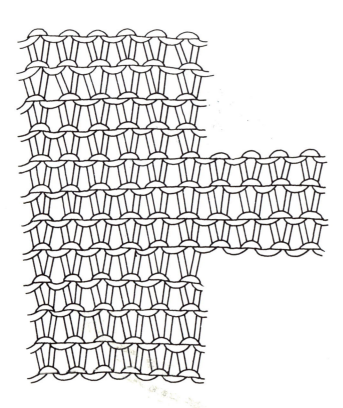

2-12.

The casting-on and binding-off method can be combined with others described in this chapter to obtain a variety of shapes. Together with a triangle, for example, a treelike form can be produced (see Figure 2-13). With the same twenty stitches, work a few inches of either garter stitch or stockinette stitch. Cast on ten stitches at the beginning of the next row, work across, turn, cast on ten more stitches, and work across. On the following row, knit the first two stitches together, work across the row, knit the last two stitches together, and knit back. Decrease in this manner on every other row nine more times to return to the original twenty stitches (Figure 2-14). Continue until the desired length is reached.

Try this and other combinations with different sizes of needles. You don't have to cast on or bind off the same number of stitches on each side every time. You'll be enchanted by the variety of shapes that you can come up with. I often start a knit-art project with one idea in mind, change methods in midstream, and end up with something totally unanticipated — my very own creation. If a design pleases you, that's what counts.

2-13. *Tree*. (Photograph by Roy Goodall)

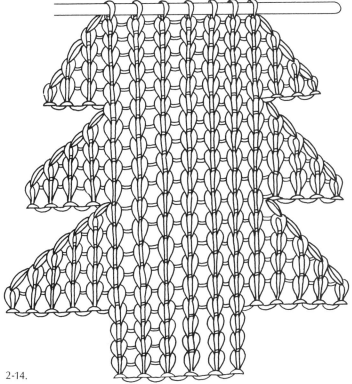

2-14.

BIAS KNITTING

Since visually stimulating shapes are the basis for an artistic approach to knitting, it is important to know how to knit on the bias.

Bias knitting can be done with any number of stitches and in garter stitch, stockinette stitch, or pattern stitch. To slant your work to the right, cast on twenty or thirty stitches, and work across the row. On the next row, increase one stitch in the first stitch, work across the row, and knit the last two stitches together. Turn and work straight back. Continue in this manner on every other row, increasing in the first stitch and decreasing at the end of the same row, until you have the desired length (see Figure 2-15).

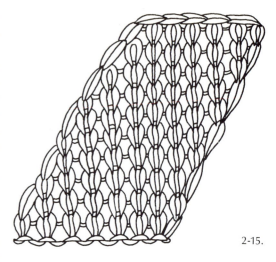

2-15.

To slant your work in the opposite direction, reverse the procedure, knitting the first two stitches together and increasing one stitch in the last stitch (Figure 2-16). Remember to increase and decrease only on every other row — this is what makes the bias.

To make right and left biases on the same piece (see Figure 2-17), proceed as follows:

Cast on thirty stitches, and work even for several rows. On the next row, increase one stitch in the first stitch, work across twelve more stitches, and knit the next two stitches together. Put the remaining fifteen stitches on a holder. Work back and forth on the fifteen stitches on the needle as described above for two or three inches (enough to see the direction easily). Put these stitches on a holder. Attach another ball of yarn, and work the bias in the opposite direction. To bring the bias pieces together, work the right bias to the left and the left bias to the right for the same number of inches. Break off one ball of yarn, and knit across all thirty stitches. Notice that the two meet at the center to form a diamond-shaped opening (Figure 2-18); the outer edges are saw-toothed.

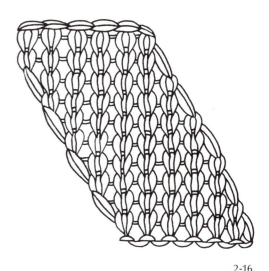

2-16.

To make a triangle shape (Figure 2-19), work the bias pieces in opposite directions as explained above. To form the triangle, work across the first fifteen stitches, cast on ten stitches, and work across the remaining fifteen stitches.

Any type or combination of bias knitting can be inserted anywhere in a design. The effect can be heightened by knitting each bias segment in a different color (Figure 2-20). As the designer, experiment until you find just the right combination. As you continue to explore different shapes and patterns, you will discover many new ways to add interest to your work.

2-17.

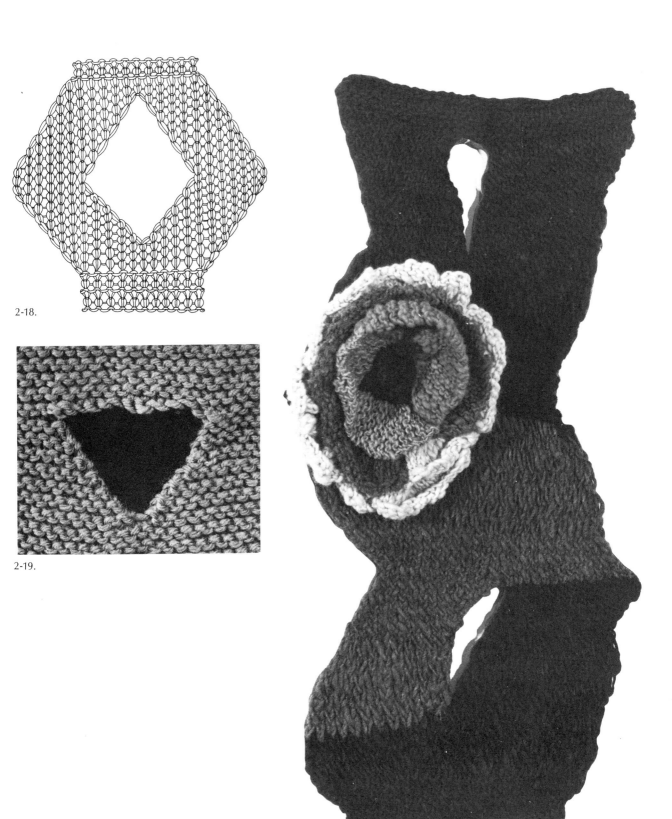

2-18.

2-19.

2-20. *Flower*. Background knitted on the bias in shades of charcoal and brown handspun wool and mounted on ¾" plywood. The flower is composed of garter-stitch strips in yellow, red, blue, orange, and pink vegetable-dyed handspun wool. 40" long x 20" wide. (Photograph by Roy Goodall)

HOLES AND OPENINGS

At some point in your piece, you may want to make an opening, if for no other reason than to break up the solid sections (see Figure C-3). Open areas can dramatize your work by introducing another color or texture. An internationally known interior designer once said that no design element is so intriguing as one that lets you "see through."

To make a simple opening, start with forty stitches, and work the usual few rows of garter stitch to emphasize the new area. Following Figure 2-21, work across twelve stitches on the next row, and slip the remaining stitches onto a holder. Working back and forth on these twelve stitches, *decrease* one stitch on every other row six times on the side where you made the division, ending on the reverse side. Then, on the same edge, *increase* one stitch on every other row six times so that you again have twelve stitches. Break the yarn, leaving a piece about five inches long to be woven in later, and slip these twelve stitches onto a holder.

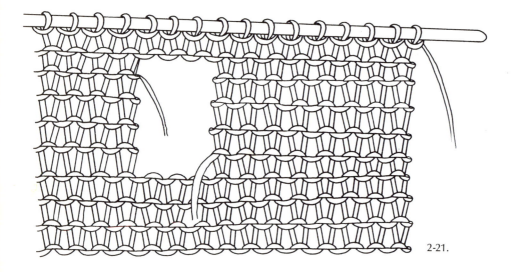

2-21.

Slip the stitches from the first holder to your needle, and tie on your ball of yarn. With the same sequence of increasing and decreasing, work the second piece to correspond to the first. Be careful to decrease and increase at the division of your work, ending at the outer edge.

To join the two segments, slip the twelve stitches from the holder to the needle carrying the rest of the stitches, and work across all forty stitches. Don't be alarmed if the stitches are rather loose at the juncture point; these can be concealed when you finish the piece.

By varying the number of rows between increases and decreases, you can create many more shapes (see Figures C-4 and C-5). For instance, after dividing your work at any point, decrease and increase on only *one* side. Or decrease and increase on *every* row rather than every *other* row. Try this technique with two different sizes of needles or two different colors. Or knit one side in garter stitch and the other in stockinette stitch. Many different interior shapes can be achieved with these simple variations.

For a more regular, rectangular opening, proceed this way: on about forty stitches, work two or three inches in stockinette stitch, ending with a purl row. On the next row, knit across fifteen stitches, and slip these onto a holder. Bind off the first five of the remaining stitches, and complete the row. Work back and forth on these stitches until you have about two inches, and end with a purl row. Slip these stitches on a holder, and break the yarn, leaving a six-inch strand. Slip the fifteen stitches from the first holder to the needle, and work back and forth until this piece measures the same length as the first, again ending with a purl row. On the next row, knit fifteen stitches, cast on five stitches, and then knit the stitches from the second holder. Work back and forth for three or four rows in stockinette stitch to join your work.

As you continue experimenting, you will discover how easy it is to make many kinds of openings. It is fun to scatter these randomly through your work and to introduce other materials, such as twigs or flowers, in the spaces thus created.

SLITS

You can also weave decorative objects through slits in your work (see Figure 2-22). These slits can be made in a regular or irregular sequence. Work across six or eight stitches, bind off four stitches, and complete the row. On the next row, cast on four stitches over the bound-off stitches, and finish the row. Don't be afraid to insert slits wherever it pleases you.

2-22.

CIRCULAR KNITTING

Just as changing needle sizes or changing colors can stimulate the imagination, changing direction can do so as well. One of the best ways to create a three-dimensional appearance is to knit in the round. This eliminates seams, which can easily detract from the pattern continuity. There are two basic methods: one with circular needles, the other with four double-pointed or sock needles.

CIRCULAR NEEDLES

Cast on about sixty stitches (enough to go around your circular needle). Be careful to keep the stitches straight on the needle. To join the stitches, place a marker (a piece of yarn in a different color, a safety pin, or a plastic marker) on the right-hand needle. Now, holding your needles as in Figure 2-23, knit the first stitch on the left-hand needle, and continue knitting all the stitches until you come back to the marker again. This completes one row. Make sure that you don't twist the stitches or knit the marker. Slide the marker over to the right-hand needle, and continue knitting. Remember, you are always working with the right side facing you in circular knitting.

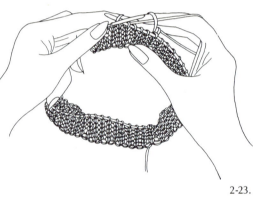

2-23.

2-24. Detail of *Venturi* (see Figure C-6). (Photograph by Roy Goodall)

Knit up four or five inches in this manner. To make the mushroomlike form shown in Figure 2-24, increase one stitch every sixth stitch all the way around the next row. If you started with sixty stitches, for example, add ten more stitches. Knit four rows even, then increase one stitch every seventh stitch. This adds ten more stitches. Increase in this way until you achieve the desired circumference. Work one row of purl stitch as a starting point for the decreasing process. (Circular work that is knitted on every row looks like stockinette stitch.) On the next row, begin to decrease in the reverse sequence, with the same number of rows between each row of decreasing, until you reach the original number of stitches.

This is only a guideline for increasing and decreasing in the round. Experiment with other variations, perhaps increasing every third stitch or every stitch, to see what kinds of effects are possible. Try knitting in the back of the stitch, alternating a row of knitting with a row of purling, or a simple pattern stitch.

The free-hanging sculpture in Figure C-6 shows the versatility of circular knitting. It was knitted with sizes 9, 11, and 13 circular needles, changing to the next larger needle every four rows or so, and at the same time increasing and decreasing at spaced intervals. The slender tubes separating the mushroomlike forms were knitted with double-pointed needles.

2-25.

DOUBLE-POINTED NEEDLES

This method of circular knitting requires four double-pointed needles. In order to accustom your fingers to four separate needles, practice by casting on fifteen stitches apiece from the same strand of yarn on three of the needles. Place a marker on the fourth needle, and knit the first cast-on stitch on the first needle. Continue to knit around as shown in Figure 2-25.

The four-needle method might seem clumsy in comparison with the circular-needle method. With double-pointed needles, however, it is possible to knit very narrow, tubular pieces (see Figure C-7). Even though you may not use these double-pointed needles often, they are well worth mastering.

STRAIGHT NEEDLES

If you don't mind seams, you can fake circular knitting by increasing and decreasing on straight needles. Knit two separate but identical curved pieces, adding and subtracting stitches as already described, then sew the two pieces together. You will have side seams, but if you weave them together carefully with needle and yarn, they won't be noticeable. Alternatively, you can make these seams an important part of your design (see Chapter 9) or divide your fabric into several parts and seam them together.

SQUARES AND RECTANGLES

Throughout this chapter you've been playing with all kinds of shapes — diamond, oval, triangular, and circular. But don't forget the most common shapes — rectangles and squares. A long, rectangular hanging can be very beautiful; all you need to do is to combine an interesting fiber, a simple stitch, possibly some beads, a bit of fringe to polish it off, and a good-looking rod.

The rectangular hanging in Figure 2-26 shows how lovely utter simplicity can be. Crossed insertion, wrap stitch, garter stitch, and grand eyelet lace (see Chapter 5) were knitted with a size 19 needle in irregular sequences. Plastic beads in a regular pattern were inserted in the large garter-stitch areas (see Chapter 6) and included as part of the fringe. The piece can either hang freely (it is the same on both sides) or on a wall.

A square is perhaps the least difficult of all shapes to knit. But what you do with it is totally up to your own imagination. In Figure 2-27, a square was turned into a diamond, and a separately knitted bias piece was sewn on the surface. The piece was knitted on size 15 needles in that old standby, garter stitch. This small hanging utilizes all the elements of design — color, shape, line, and form — in an easy but effective way. Try something similar when you're in the mood for instant knit art.

So much for shapes, but let me add a word of caution. Although there is a more comprehensive discussion of fibers and yarns in Chapter 4, it is worth mentioning at the outset that linen, cotton, jute, and leather are the most satisfactory materials for a large, free-hanging piece, because they do not have much stretch. Wool fibers have a tendency to sag, especially in larger hangings, unless they are combined with a more stable yarn, such as cotton or linen. Let your common sense be your guide.

By now it should be evident that knit art is not concise; that the shapes described here are meant to trigger further explorations; that any and all combinations are possible.

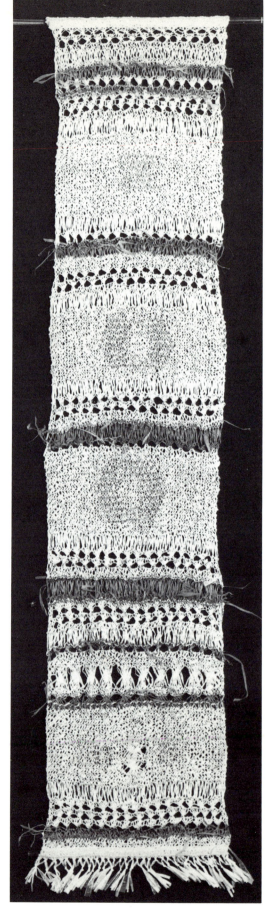

2-26. *Plastique II.* Hanging, knitted in opaque plastic twine and burnt-orange raffia and trimmed with beads and a fringe. 108″ long x 24″ wide. (Photograph by Mike Sedam)

2-27. *Orientale*. Hanging, knitted in rayon and cotton rug yarn, trimmed with wooden beads and brass temple bells from India, and hung with a Japanese medallion. (Photograph by Mike Sedam)

3.
COLOR IT

The color of a piece can be either the most predominant characteristic or a complement to another unusual feature of the design. If the color is making the strongest impact, it is what you notice first when your creation is hanging. In that case, you should minimize the texture of the yarn or fiber and of the pattern and emphasize the shape or form alone. For instance, if you decide to use bright pink and blue, as in Figure 3-1, an irregular edge would be appropriate, but choose a simple knitting technique in order not to detract from the bold colors. Garter stitch or stockinette stitch would be quite suitable. In other words, if color and texture have equal status, they will compete.

On the other hand, if you are working with a lovely natural fiber such as handspun wool or linen, you should emphasize its texture by using a subtle color, perhaps its natural color. Figure 3-2 was knitted with two shades of purple jute, which give the piece a soft glow and emphasize its round form. Jute has only a slight surface texture, so stockinette stitch was used throughout in order not to interfere with it. Figure 3-3 is a good arrangement of several shades of blue and blue-green wool and rayon, each with a different texture but all working together.

I urge you to rely on your personal taste; you don't have to follow any rules of color combination. Begin to relate everything around you to color, from the many hues of nature to a lovely piece of material. Think about what gives you pleasure — the soft blues, pinks, and grays of the sky; the bright reds and oranges of a sunrise or sunset; the muted noncolors of pebbles on the beach. A whole new world of color will open up, and your senses will become so sharpened that you will want to immediately transfer these perceptions to your knitting needles.

3-1. Hanging, knitted in blue, white, and pink polypropylene fiber. Knitted by a student of Rosalie King, University of Washington. (Photograph by Mary Jane Anderson)

3-2. *Purpl-xd*. Free-hanging, three-dimensional sculpture, knitted in jute and trimmed with wooden beads. Stockinette stitch, garter stitch, and double knitting on size 17 needles. (Photograph by Roy Goodall)

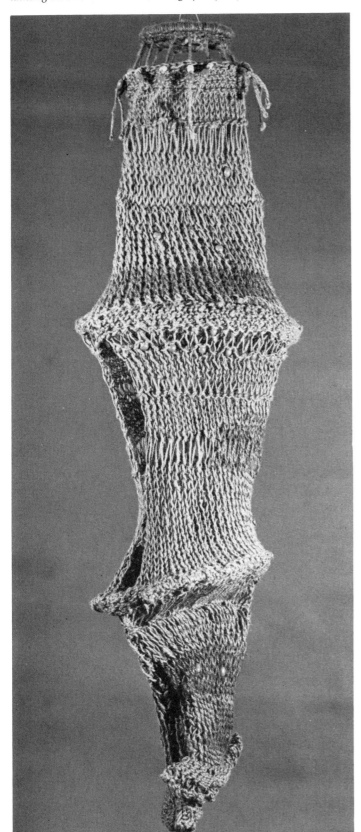

3-3. *Knit Dreams*. Bas-relief hanging, made in a wool and wool/rayon blend. Knitted by Mary Scott. (Photograph by Mary Scott)

Whether or not you're conscious of it, color strongly influences your daily life. Therefore, it is wise to work with colors you are comfortable with, even down to the color of your needles. You certainly don't want to start a project in a color that doesn't particularly excite you but that you force yourself to work with day after day. On the other hand, don't be timid; as you get more involved, you'll combine colors that you might not have considered compatible before. Visit some craft shops and art galleries to see how other artists use color. Their work may stimulate new ideas of your own.

If you are unsure of a color scheme, take the time to lay out several strands on a flat surface. Move them around in different combinations. This will enable you to determine whether or not the colors go together and may save you many hours of ripping later on.

It is useful to make a color card of all the fibers and yarns that you have, grouping those in the same color family together. Leave space for new acquisitions. Staple these samples to a piece of cardboard, and as you obtain additional fibers, add them to the color card with the proper identification.

Two or more colors worked alternately can present a real challenge (see Figure 3-4). In free-form knitting, it's fun to join another color whimsically somewhere in the body of your work. For instance, if your major color is a bright green and you would like to introduce a blob of white, drop the green and begin knitting with the white over several stitches. Drop the white, and, with a new ball of green, work the rest of the stitches on the row. On the next row, work back with the green, drop that strand, work with the white over the originally designated stitches, drop the white, and continue with the green. Work back and forth in this manner over as many rows as are necessary for your design. Then continue working with your major color. You will have several loose strands and a larger-than-usual hole where you have introduced the new color. Don't be too concerned; these strands can be woven in later, but be sure to weave the joined strands back into the same color so they are not visible from the front of your fabric.

When you work with more than one color along an entire row, it is important to carry the additional colors *loosely* across the back of the piece. I recommend twisting them into the working yarn every two stitches in order to retain an even tension and to avoid distorting the pattern. Pick up the new color from underneath; this eliminates a hole where one color ends and the other begins. If you are working with several colors at once, it is a good idea to wind each on a bobbin (you can buy these at yarn shops) or a piece of cardboard to avoid tangling.

Soft toys may be considered a form of knit art. Figure 3-5 was knitted in green, navy, bright red, and purple knitting worsted. Notice that the wings were shaped by increasing at the outer edges. The body was made of yellow satin, stuffed, and a blob of orange satin was added for the head.

3-4. *Moheraldry*. Hanging, knitted of multicolor mohair. Stockinette stitch and garter stitch with overlaid bias strips and protruding tubular forms. Knitted by Mary Scott. (Photograph by Mary Scott)

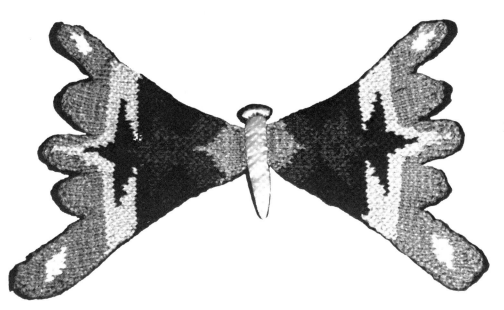

3-5. *Butterfly*. Made in knitting worsted and satin. Knitted by Margaret Swanson-Vance.

Figure 3-6 is simply a tube made of knitting worsted and stuffed. Lines of different colors were incorporated in the tube, and bright, shiny buttons were added for eyes.

Overlaying and appliquéing are other ways of introducing color. Knit a separate shape and lay it right on the face of your fabric. It can then be sewn on with the same color yarn to make the stitching unobtrusive or else appliquéd in a different color with a decorative embroidery stitch. These methods are less complicated than working two colors at once, since you can knit any shape and attach it to the fabric. Layers of different colors and different shapes can be overlaid, one on top of the other, leaving small sections of each color exposed. Perhaps a more regular pattern of color is more suitable for your purposes; lay the pieces out side by side or in any other manner. The bright blue overlay in Figure C-8 was knitted by increasing and decreasing irregularly (see Chapter 2), then sewn to the sculpture with a matching-color yarn after it was stuffed.

A multicolored fabric is an effective background for solid-color patches. To obtain this tweed effect, combine two, three, four, or more strands of different colors.

Think of knit art as painting with yarn and knitting needles. There are no limits to the combinations of colors and no restrictions as to how or when you introduce them. Color can make a shape come alive or become the catalyst for your design.

3-6. *Snake*. Sculpture in stuffed knitting worsted. Stockinette stitch. Knitted by Margaret Swanson-Vance.

4.

MATERIALS MATTER

Knitting is usually associated with conventional yarns such as knitting worsted (medium-weight, flat wool) or dress yarns (usually a finer weight), but there is a whole world of cords, strings, leather, and even wire that can be manipulated around a pair of knitting needles. Plastic twine, ordinarily used by printers for tying bundles, has a glossy texture, and, together with conventional fibers, can produce a wall hanging of real beauty (see Figure 4-1). The heavy, waxed linen often used for macramé looks and feels exactly right for a three-dimensional hanging (see Figures 4-2 and 4-3). It was a chore maneuvering this fiber over and under the needles, but the challenge actually stimulated the design.

Any or all of the above-mentioned fibers may be combined successfully, and your imagination is the only limit to their usefulness. Again, I urge you to look in unusual places for these materials; you'll be pleasantly surprised by how much is available.

For example, a marine-supply depot proved to be a gold mine of cords and ropes in an infinite number of sizes and textures, and in cotton, synthetics, and blends. They may be purchased in small amounts or in whole reels. Hardware and surplus stores are great places for scrounging.

Further exploration during a trip to Hawaii led me to discover *hau* fiber, ordinarily used for basket weaving. The sample shown in Figure 4-4 was knitted on size 35 needles, and because the material was neither smooth nor in a continuous strand, the raw ends were left wherever they occurred. The surface texture that resulted was most appealing and different, so I left it as it was.

Craft magazines usually carry advertisements from yarn distributors. Shops that sell weavers' supplies are also good sources. For a small charge to cover handling and mailing, most of these places will send color cards showing their stock.

4-1. *Plastique I.* Hanging, knitted in opaque plastic twine and cotton cord on size 13 needles, with hand-polished Japanese rocks inserted in pockets, and trimmed with glass beads. 84″ long x 12″ wide. (Collection of Mr. and Mrs. Gerald Cone; photograph by Roy Goodall)

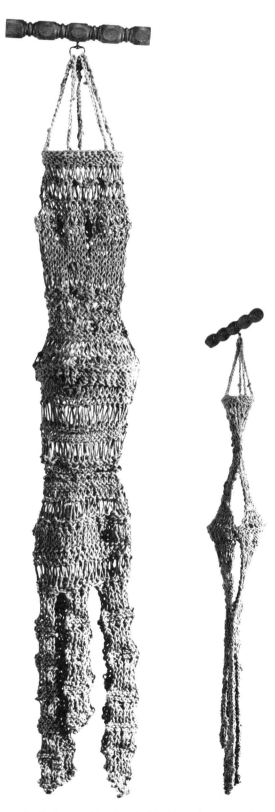

4-2 and 4-3. *Skeletons.* Hanging, knitted in natural waxed linen and trimmed with leather, glass balls, and hand-polished rocks. Double knitting and garter stitch on size 19 needles. 60″ long x 12″ wide. (Photograph by Roy Goodall)

Long-time knitters will probably have odds and ends left over from other projects. Here's an opportunity to put these to work. Some of the most intriguing things done by my workshop students were contrived from the imaginative use of leftovers.

In your explorations of new fibers you'll discover that the variety is unlimited — linen, wool, cotton, a multitude of synthetics, blends of synthetics and natural fibers, and probably many more that I haven't mentioned. You can use two or more fibers in one piece to increase the possibilities even further. One of my favorites is a strong, flat linen, which I often use in combination with homespun wool. The linen is strong and adds the stability that the soft wool requires, particularly for a large hanging. The wool by itself tends to stretch when hung; the linen helps to retard that stretch. In Figure 4-5, double-strand wool rug yarn from Sweden was used, and although I hadn't thought seriously about the basic properties of the yarn (I just liked its color and feel), I soon discovered that the natural sag that occurred simply from hanging produced far more interesting proportions.

Other fun fibers to try are cowhair, horsehair, goathair, and even human hair. I should warn you that horsehair sheds badly, leaves a greasy film on your hands, and has an odor which I find rather unpleasant. In spite of these disadvantages, I like the effect that it produced in Figure C-9. The horsehair was used for the long fingerlike areas, and it contrasted strongly with the sisal-wrapped hula hoops. Heavy homespun wool, left to its own devices, was interjected into the crocheted, amoebic sisal forms and attached to the hoops. As you see, three totally different but compatible natural fibers were combined.

4-4.

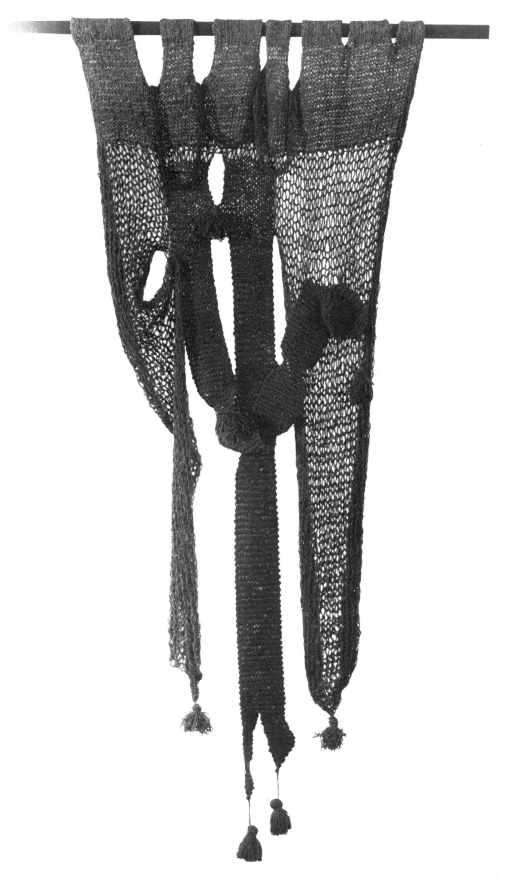

4-5. *Caverns*. Hanging, knitted in double strands in charcoal, maroon, and dark green Swedish rug wool. Stockinette stitch on size 15 needles. 120" long x 60" wide. (Photograph by Mike Sedam)

New yarns are lovely to use, but think about reusing old afghans or out-of-date knitted wearables. Even old blankets can be cut into strips and knitted. As you rip, wrap the yarn around a large piece of cardboard (Figure 4-6) or a large book, and tie it securely. You will have a hank or skein, which is much easier to work with. The yarn will be crinkly from previous use, so dip it carefully in lukewarm, gentle suds. I prefer one of the liquid soaps made especially for laundering wool. Rinse carefully two or three times to remove all the soap, squeeze the water out, and lay the hank on a terry towel to dry. When it is almost dry, shake it and hang it up over a covered hanger so that the air will circulate through all the strands for more even drying. When it is thoroughly dry, wind loosely in a ball (Figure 4-7).

Too lazy to wash your recycled yarn? After you've made the hank, slip it over the end of your ironing board, and lightly steam out the wrinkles with an iron. And if you are even lazier than that, use it as is with all the crinkles (Figure 4-8). I've come up with some crazy textures by doing just that, because each yarn or fiber reacts differently.

Many yarns are not prewound, so you may want to invest in a yarn winder simply to save time when your fingers are itching to get started. Yarn winders are usually sold at yarn shops or weaving studios. They come in two sizes, and they are most often made of wood. Although electric winders are available, they tend to break down frequently. Two chairs, back to back, will work just as well for winding yarn (Figure 4-9). Or you can simply drape the yarn around your knees. In any case, yarn-winding time can be well spent by thinking about your ultimate design.

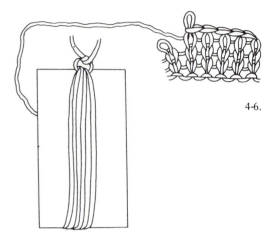

4-6.

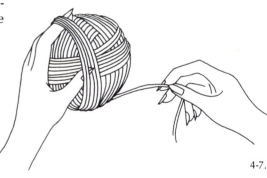

4-7.

4-8.

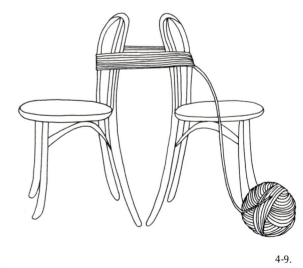

4-9.

The more you discover about the individual properties of various fibers and yarns, the more enjoyment you will derive from your knitting. They can do marvelous things; to become familiar with their behavior and possibilities, you should acquire samples of some of the fibers discussed in this chapter and knit a few inches on several sizes of needles. Feel the fibers, soak them, pull them before beginning a serious piece of work.

With your notebook nearby to record the results, soak the fibers in water, and leave them to dry. Observe whether they shrink, stretch, or shrivel. Pull on them to see if the strands become distorted. Apply steam lightly, and move the fibers with your fingers to learn which ones harden, which ones soften. What you find out is of tremendous importance in determining what to knit and how to knit it, and which fibers can be worked together agreeably.

Cotton or linen should first be laid out on a flat surface. (Strong cardboard cutting boards are inexpensive and readily available at fabric shops.) Fasten the edges firmly to the board with T-pins, and steam them lightly with a steam iron (Figure 4-10). To avoid a hard-pressed look, hold the iron an inch or two above the material, and smooth out the material with your fingers. (Be careful not to burn yourself with the hot steam!) Leave the material pinned to the board until it is dry.

Cotton, linen, jute, and other natural fibers can usually be stretched quite successfully. If you have an old-fashioned curtain stretcher hidden away in a closet, now is the time to pull it out. Fasten the material to the stretcher carefully to avoid stretcher ridges. Spray with water, and let dry. If you feel that the material needs more body, spray it with a commercial spray starch that leaves no white residue.

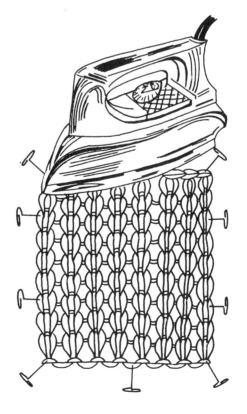

4-10.

For even more firmness, I often use Make-a-Shade, a do-it-yourself laminating product that also comes in a spray can. It is ordinarily used for laminating woven fabric to plain window shades, but I've found it especially useful for knit art. It won't change the texture or the color of most fibers, but it's a good idea to spray a small sample first just for insurance. The fumes are strong, so be sure to use it in a well-ventilated room, or better still, outdoors. Be sure to read the directions on the can. Pin the fabric wrong side out to the board with T-pins. Spray completely, and allow to dry for about an hour. Turn it over carefully, pin it down again, and spray once more. To firm up a free-hanging circular construction, stand back ten or twelve inches and spray up and down as you walk around it. When the fabric is completely dry to the touch (not sticky), spray again. Usually this is enough. However, if you prefer a more rigid finish, another coat or two won't harm the fabric. Not only does Make-a-Shade add strength to the material, but it also helps to deter soil.

Heat should not be applied to synthetics or synthetic blends. It is usually sufficient to moisten them lightly and pin them to a flat surface until they are dry.

Leather lacing (see Figure 4-11) will probably need some adjusting after it has been knitted. Lightly sprinkle a swatch of the leather with water. Cover it with heavy brown paper (used grocery bags will do), and steam it carefully, using almost no pressure in order not to flatten the leather.

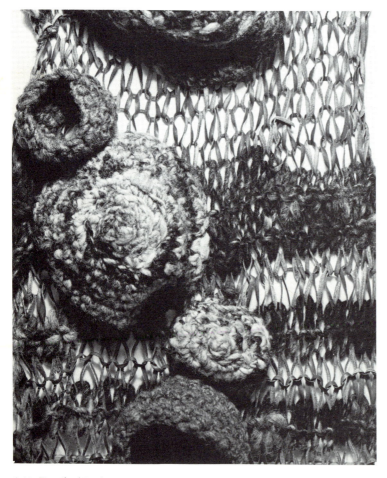

4-11. Detail of *Earth* (see Figure 10-7). (Photograph by Roy Goodall)

Soft, lovely, flexible wool is the crème de la crème of fibers and the material that I most enjoy working with. You should be aware of its characteristics, however, especially when knitting wall hangings. Wool is a natural fiber that has a great deal of elasticity, so if you are planning a large-scale wall piece, remember that there will be a certain amount of sag just in the hanging. If your piece is very heavy, it might conceivably stretch several inches from its original size; accommodate your design accordingly. Furthermore, unless you intend to anchor the edges in some way, perhaps with a facing, the weight of the yarn tends to make the edges curl (see Figure 4-12). If you like this effect, don't spray or block the fabric — just let it go.

Rayon yarns can be soft or coarse, smooth or slubbed, thick or thin, and they often have a sheen which contrasts interestingly with fluffy wool or rough jute. Rayon also makes a good stabilizer for more flexible fibers.

Silk is another beautiful yarn, but it is expensive and limited in supply. It has three characteristics that make it very exciting to work with: its natural sheen, its strength, and its flexibility. It rarely needs more than very light steaming. Handle it carefully — it's precious!

Raffia is another natural fiber with somewhat the same properties as the *hau* fiber mentioned in Chapter 4, although it is less brittle. Frequent joining is necessary because of its uneven length, but this can give an unusual quality to your fabric. It is available in a wide variety of colors.

Cotton or cotton-and-synthetic-blend strings and cords are satisfactory fibers for knit art, and they are relatively inexpensive. The intermediate ropes, such as those used by sailors, call for very large needles and result in a more open weave.

Because knit art is spontaneous and you will be creating as you go along, there is no prescribed method of determining the exact amount of material you will need. I suggest you buy a small amount, knit a few inches, then measure vertically and horizontally. This will give you a fairly good idea of how far a particular amount of yarn or fiber will go. Then try to anticipate how large your completed project will be. This will help you make an educated guess as to how much to buy initially. Then buy an extra amount for emergency — it's always better to have too much than too little, and whatever is left over can be used for something else. Fortunately, because knit art is not that precise, you need not be overly concerned about color variations in dye lots. Slight color variations might prove more interesting. It will help if you keep a record of your findings for future use.

Another whole book could be written about the infinite kinds of materials available and how to use them. I hope that these suggestions will encourage you to be alert for others not mentioned and that you will not hesitate to try them.

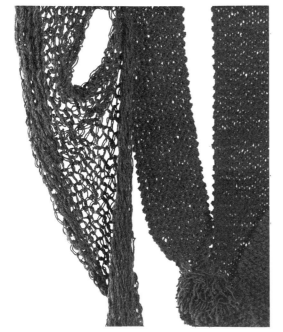

4-12. Detail of *Caverns* (see Figure 4-5). (Photograph by Mike Sedam)

5.

YOU'RE IN STITCHES

The stitches in a knitted structure are obviously important, but, in my opinion, they are only the means to an end. Most of the examples shown rely on the basic stitches, garter stitch and stockinette stitch, sometimes exaggerating, sometimes minimizing them. I am excited by the materials themselves, and I like to work without a preconceived notion of the finished product, so I prefer not to be bogged down with remembering the number of stitches and rows in a particular pattern. Some designs, however, are enhanced by the intricacy of a more complicated pattern stitch, and a change of pace within your work is often refreshing.

As with anything, the more you know, the more you may take poetic license. Mastery of the formal structures opens up new areas for improvisation. There are hundreds of specific pattern stitches. Those included here are among the simplest, yet they provide many opportunities for textural variation.

As with your other experiments, it is a good idea to attach an identifying tag to these samples for future reference. One of my friends makes a swatch of each of her pattern stitches, mounts them in a cardboard frame, and writes all the pertinent information on the back. She not only has a visual reference, but the result is handsome enough to hang on the wall.

5-1.

PURSE STITCH

The *purse stitch* (Figure 5-1) is an openwork stitch; it is especially dramatic in a divider or screen. It has a lacy appearance when worked in a fine yarn or cord on a large needle (size 13 or even 35). A bulkier yarn produces a tighter fabric. Try the stitch on several different sizes of needles and with different weights of yarn (perhaps in two colors, with a third color for the in-between areas) to see how the pattern changes. On an even number of stitches, the formula is as follows:

Row 1: K1 (edge st); *yo, p2 tog*; repeat from * to *; k1 (edge st).

The stitch has only one row to the pattern, which is repeated over and over and back and forth on every row, so it is easy to remember.

LOOP STITCH

Another stitch you will enjoy is the *loop stitch* (Figure 5-2). The pattern (Figure 5-3), worked with any number of stitches, is as follows:

Row 1: K1 (edge st); *put right-hand needle in first st on left-hand needle, pass the yarn around the right-hand needle as for knitting, wind the yarn around your index finger and needles twice, and knit off the three loops together in the usual way*; work every stitch in this manner.

Row 2: *K, working three threads in each st.*

This stitch does require watching, and again, you should practice it on several needle sizes and in several thicknesses of yarn until you get the hang of it. A couple of rows of garter stitch or stockinette stitch between the loop rows will keep the fabric from becoming too stiff and hard to handle. Notice also that the loops appear on the opposite side of your work. For a more lush appearance, use two strands of yarn together. Leave the loops as is or cut them for a shaggy finish when you are through.

5-2. Detail of *Orientale* (see Figure 2-27). Garter stitch and loop stitch. (Photograph by Mike Sedam)

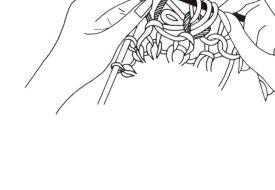

5-3.

WOVEN BASKET STITCH

The *woven basket stitch* (Figure 5-4) is a rather firm weave that contrasts well with large, open areas. On an even number of stitches:

Row 1: *Pass the right-hand needle behind the first st on the left-hand needle, k second st, k first st in usual way*.

Row 2: P1; *p the second st, p the first st*; p1.

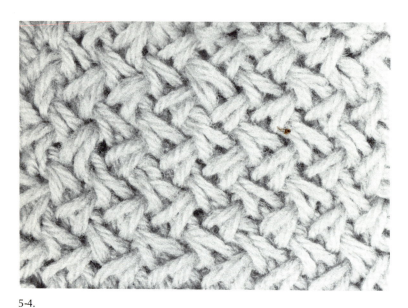

5-4.

WRAP STITCH

The *wrap stitch* is one of the most versatile and simple pattern stitches, so I find myself using it frequently. It is merely an exaggerated stockinette or garter stitch, but the length of the stitch can be controlled by the number of wraps. It is worked on any number of stitches, as shown in Figure 5-5:

Row 1: *K, winding yarn around the needle three times.*

Row 2: *K or p, letting the extra wraps drop.*

Make sure to use long enough needles for this pattern: two extra loops are added to each stitch on your needle, thereby tripling the number of stitches temporarily. For example, if you start with twenty stitches, the wraps increase the number of loops to sixty. The wrap stitch can be done on either the knit or the purl side of your work. If you use a circular needle, separate the two rows of pattern by a row or two of garter or stockinette stitch (see Figure C-10). The number of wraps may be increased or decreased, depending on how large an open stitch you prefer (see Figure 5-6).

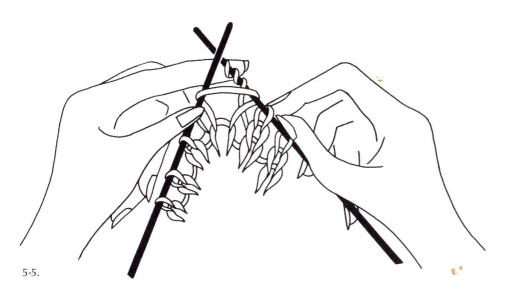

5-5.

5-6. (Above) Three wraps. (Below) Two wraps. (Photograph by Roy Goodall)

TWISTED STOCKINETTE STITCH

The *twisted stockinette stitch* (Figures 5-7 and 5-8) is a variation of the stockinette stitch, which relieves the boredom of plain knitting and has a slightly firmer texture. The directions are simple:

Row 1: *Kb*.
Row 2: *P*.

5-7.

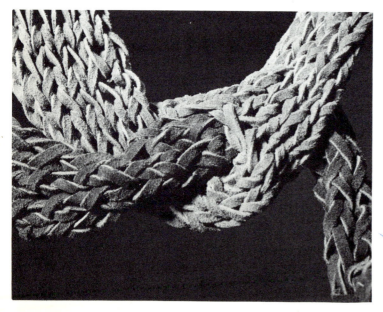

5-8. Detail of *Naturals Again* (see Figure 6-1). Twisted stockinette stitch. (Photograph by Roy Goodall)

CROSSED INSERTION

A *crossed insertion* (Figure 5-9), also known as *Indian cross-stitch*, is a piquant way of indicating semiopen areas. The stitch is not difficult, but be careful not to twist the crossed stitches when transferring them from one needle to the other. This pattern is worked on an even number of stitches in multiples of six. *Multiple* means that each pattern group contains six stitches (and that the total number of stitches must be divisible by six). If you like, add a stitch or two at each edge as a border, but remember not to include them in your pattern. The sequence is as follows:

Row 1: *K1, wrapping thread around the right-hand needle twice*; continue this across the row.

Row 2: *Sl 3 onto a cable needle (a double-pointed needle or a bobby pin will do as well), (letting the extra loop drop) k3, (letting the extra loop drop) k3 from cable needle.*

You can make the pattern larger or smaller by varying the number of crossed stitches (Figure 5-10), but add or subtract in multiples of two (instead of six stitches, use eight or four, for example).

5-9. Detail of *Plastique II* (see Figure 2-26). Crossed insertions. (Photograph by Mike Sedam)

5-10. Wall hanging, knitted in linen. Crossed insertions. 45″ long x 36″ wide. Knitted by Ivarose Bovingdon. (Photograph by Margaret Broughton)

SEED STITCH

The *seed stitch* (Figure 5-11), sometimes referred to as *moss stitch,* is a low-key, allover pattern, which gives your fabric a pebbled look and feel. It is ridiculously easy to do:

Row 1: On an even number of sts, *k1, p1* across the row.
Row 2: *P1, k1*.

Always begin the second row of the pattern with the same stitch that ended the previous row; if you ended with a knit stitch, for example, begin the next row with a knit stitch. If you want to add stitches at the beginning or end of a row, keep the above formula in mind so that you retain the pattern structure. This holds true whether you are working on a straight piece of fabric or on the bias.

5-11.

GRAND EYELET LACE

Worked in a fine yarn on a medium-sized needle, *grand eyelet lace* (Figure 5-12) is a filmy, openwork pattern stitch. It requires just four stitches to each pattern grouping and three rows to complete the pattern. Yarn overs are part of the pattern, so be careful not to lose that extra *made* stitch:

Row 1: On an even number of sts, *yo, p4 tog*; repeat * to *.
Row 2: *K1, (k1, p1, k1) into the yo of the previous row*; repeat * to *.
Row 3: K.

5-12.

5-13.

CAT'S EYE

Another allover lacy pattern that changes character when done with different sizes of needles is the *cat's eye* (Figure 5-13):

Row 1: On an even number of sts, k4 (edge sts); *(yo) twice, k4*; repeat from * to *.

Row 2: P2; *p2 tog, (p1, k1) into the 2 yo's of the previous row, p2 tog*; repeat * to *; end with p2.

Row 3: K2, yo; *k4 (yo) twice*; repeat * to *; end with k4, yo, k2.

Row 4: P3; *(p2 tog) twice, (p1,k1) into the 2 yo's of the previous row; repeat * to *; end with (p2 tog) twice, p3.

POPCORN STITCH

The *popcorn stitch* (Figure 5-14) is fun to do and can be worked individually or clustered all over your work. This bulky stitch is frequently used in those lovely Irish fisherman's sweaters, and it is easily adapted to knit art, since the effects vary with different sizes of needles. Follow the pattern in figure 5-15:

Rows 1 and 2: K.

Row 3: K3; *(k into the front and back of the same st) twice, then k into the front again, turn your work, work 4 rows st st on these 5 sts, then with the left-hand needle, take the 2nd, 3rd, 4th, and 5th sts over the 1st st*; k3.

And here is my ultrasimple version (Figure 5-16), which eliminates the rows of stockinette stitch:

Rows 1 and 2: K.

Row 3: K3 (edge sts); *k1, without slipping the lp off the left-hand needle, k into the back and front of this st five times; slip the lp off the left-hand needle and onto the right-hand needle; with the left-hand needle, sl 2nd, 3rd, 4th, and 5th sts over the 1st st*; k3 (edge sts).

The bumps may be pulled through the material on either side.

5-14.

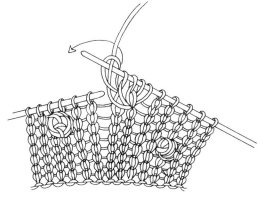

5-15.

5-16.

CABLE STITCH

The *cable stitch* is another popular stitch that often appears in Irish sweaters, and variations are showing up in all manner of handknitted objects. There are literally dozens of different types of cable stitches that you might want to check out, but the ones described here are very easy ones that don't require a cable holder.

CROSS-STITCH CABLE

The pattern in *cross-stitch cable* (Figure 5-17) has eight stitches, so the number of stitches that you cast on must be a multiple of eight, plus as many edge stitches as you desire:

Row 1: On an even number of sts, *p2, k4, p2*.

Row 2: *K2, p4, wrapping the yarn around needle twice for each p st, k2*.

Row 3: *P2, sl 4 with yarn in back, dropping the extra wrap; with left-hand needle, pass the first 2 sts over the second 2; return the sts on the right-hand needle to the left-hand needle, and k all sts in this order; p2*.

Row 4: *K2, p4, k2*.

5-17.

MOCK CABLE RIB

The mock cable rib (Figure 5-18) also has eight stitches to each sequence and is worked on an even number of stitches:

Row 1: *P5, k3*.

Row 2: *P3, k5*.

Row 3: *P5, sl 1, k2, yo, psso the k2 and the yo*.

Long, floaty strips of cable can be laid on or crisscrossed over the main part of your work for a three-dimensional effect, or you can braid them together.

Pattern stitches do require more concentration, because the design is not apparent until all the rows are worked. You may find it helpful to have someone read each step to you while you do the actual knitting or to write each pattern row on a separate card to avoid confusion while you are learning the stitches.

Any of the foregoing pattern stitches can be combined; or you can knit a large piece in one pattern stitch or scatter a series of patterns throughout for emphasis. There are so many possibilities that you'll never be at a loss for design sources. Remember to keep a record of your discoveries!

5-18.

6.

FEEL IT

Texture may well be the most important element in knit art. When I look at a wall hanging or a fiber sculpture, the urge to touch — a tingling in my fingertips — is my personal barometer for the success or failure of a piece. Sometimes the fiber itself sets off that sensation, sometimes the elevated areas. It is obviously important to incorporate interesting textural contrasts into your work.

One way to introduce textural variety is to combine different kinds of yarns and fibers or different knitting techniques in a single piece. High-low textures can be achieved by using combinations of pattern stitches (see Chapter 5). Combining an area of a flat yarn, such as linen, with another area of thick, nubby wool will create the same effect. Vary the dimensions of each area, or knit one segment on a size 8 needle and another on a size 50. For a tapestry effect, outline parts of your fabric with a simple embroidery stitch in another color. For light-and-shadow play, try alternating a flat yarn with a bulky slub yarn of a similar color.

Figure C-11 has a background of leather lacing (this is available at leather-supply houses), which was knitted in garter stitch on a size 9 and a size 19 needle used as a pair. Thick, spongy, black handspun wool added at irregular intervals provides textural relief. The volcanolike structures were formed with single crochet stitch on a large (size K) crochet hook and sewn on afterwards. They are also handspun wool, dyed in several colors with vegetable dyes. Notice that the leather background was originally rectangular but was stretched by the weight of the combined fibers.

The leather could have been worked in the round to make the form the focal point, and the wool could have been inserted in another manner to bring out the differences in texture. Other embellishments, such as beads, twigs, or fringes, do provide surface contrasts, but they can easily be overdone, and they would not be appropriate to the simple lines and materials in this design. Too much is often as bad as too little, but you have only yourself to please, so the decision is yours. Don't worry about it; just relax and have fun.

Figure 6-1 is made of suede lacing, which was knitted on the bias. Here the unusual form is paramount, but the simplicity of the mounting and the decorations emphasizes the texture of the piece.

The ribbons (gathered areas) that were described in Chapter 2 can be used to make a more regular, high-low texture, and they are easy to include. For added interest within the ribbons, you can insert some beads, metal rings, or even a pocket or two (see Chapter 7). A textured, thick-and-thin linen dress yarn provides the tactile interest in Figures 6-2 and 6-3. In addition, small, smooth, black rocks from Japan are enclosed in the pockets. A yarn-over stitch to separate the gathers and one-eight-inch clear Plexiglas rods woven through the ribbons provide several areas of interest without detracting from the oblong, monochromatic shaft.

To emphasize the subtle color changes in Figures 6-4 and 6-5, popcorns were placed at the strategic points leading into those changes. Blobs of fringe on the surface, leather pistol holders along the bottom, and three-quarter-inch Plexiglas rods painted bronze and slipped through casings (see Chapter 10) along the back of the hanging are also subtle enough not to interfere with the design. The yarn is a beautiful, primitive, dyed rug wool from Sweden.

By now I hope you have become accustomed to thinking about your knitting skills in broader terms and are developing a sense of adventure about textures — pinch, squeeze, and touch!

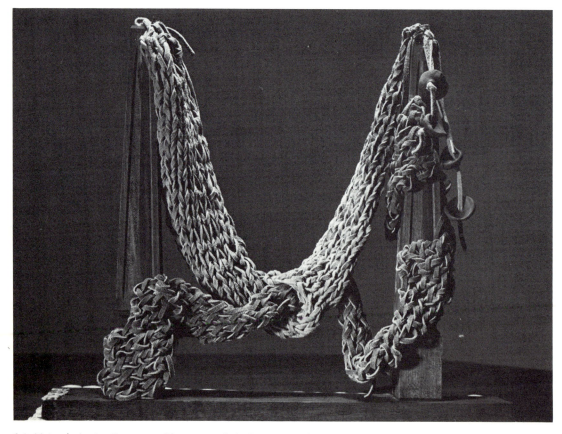

6-1. *Naturals Again*. Orange and brown suede lacing, trimmed with lava-rock beads, and mounted on a base of stained walnut. 16″ long x 12″ wide. (Collection of Mr. and Mrs. Gordon Bleil; photograph by Roy Goodall)

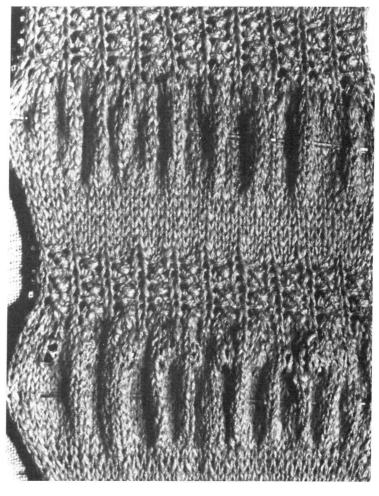

6-2 and 6-3. Hanging, knitted in slubbed linen and hung from a Plexiglas rod. 96" long x 10" wide. (Collection of Mrs. Glen Liston; photograph by Mike Sedam)

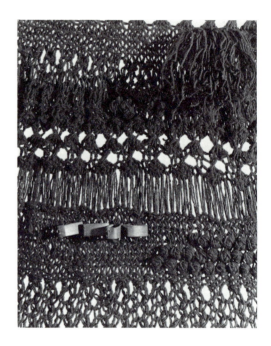

6-4 and 6-5. *Claret*. Hanging, knitted in Swedish rug wool, trimmed with leather pistol holders, and mounted on ¾″ bronze Plexiglas rods. Stockinette stitch and popcorns on size 19 needles. (Photograph by Mike Sedam)

7.

LOOK AROUND YOU

I consider found objects to be anything that can be incorporated artistically into a knitted piece. Everywhere I go, my packsack goes with me. If an object catches my eye, perhaps because of its unusual shape or color, I know that sometime, somehow, it will end up in a knitted wall hanging or sculpture. My friends are conditioned to bring me objects that they think might merit a place in my collection drawer. Start collecting; you'll be glad you did.

Beaches are fertile areas for great treasures; stray shells, lovely ocean-washed rocks, and driftwood practically jump into your hands (see Figure C-12). A bit of seaweed half-buried in the sand might suggest an unusual shape, and after drying it out, you can even include it in a knitscape to reflect the overall design. Rusty nails or odd pieces of rope can also be points of departure for a project. Don't despair if you live inland; all sorts of dried plants, flowers, and grasses make beautiful additions to knitted designs (See Figure 7-1).

Craftspeople often discard bits and pieces of wood, metal, and other materials that you can use. I always encourage my workshop students to consider anything as a possible knitting material. As long as it works for you, use it! (My only advice is to think carefully about the washability or dry-cleanability of found objects before inserting them into your work.)

7-1. Wall hanging, knitted in recycled white wool interwoven with sheaves of wheat. Knitted by a student of Rosalie King, University of Washington. (Photograph by Mary Jane Anderson)

7-2. Detail of *Skeletons* (see Figures 4-2 and 4-3). (Photograph by Roy Goodall)

For instance, in Figure 7-2 smoothly polished white rocks from Japan were slipped into a vertical series of pockets made by *double knitting*. This technique (sometimes referred to as *tubular knitting*) has many practical uses in knit art. Not only can you make pockets to hold all those rocks, twigs, pieces of driftwood, and shells that you've been gathering, but the pockets can be knitted with a different color on each side. You can, in fact, make a large, tubular wall hanging by double knitting from start to finish. The formula, always worked on an even number of stitches, is as follows:

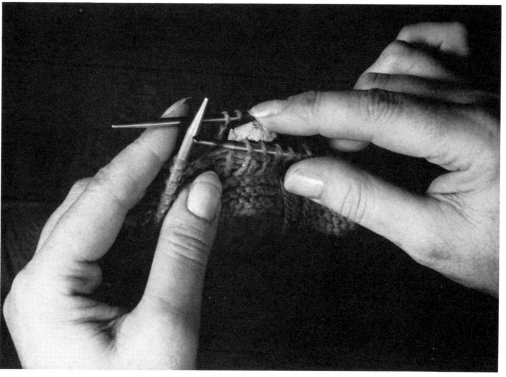

7-3.

Row 1: *K1, pull yarn to front, sl 1 as if to p, yarn in back*. Continue this over as many stitches and up as many rows as you need to accommodate the size of your object. Just be sure always to maintain an even number of stitches. To open the pocket, slip every other stitch onto a third needle, then drop in your object (see Figure 7-3). To close the pocket, put all the stitches back on the needle in *exactly* the reverse order, and knit or purl across them. Because the enclosure usually occurs within the body of your work, it helps to place markers before and after the stitches designated for the double knitting so you know precisely where the pockets begin and end. They are easily removed after you've finished.

Pockets can be stuffed with old nylons, cotton batting, or unspun wool instead of found objects. The puffed, colored jute areas in Figures 7-4 and C-13 are filled with discarded nylons (washed, naturally). Save your old bits and pieces; you never know when they might come in handy. Thrift shops also have all sorts of similar goodies stashed away in nooks and crannies, which can be purchased in large quantities at a nominal cost.

7-4. Detail of *Puff 'n Stuff* (see Figure C-13). (Photograph by Roy Goodall)

Discarded wigs are great for stuffing, and one of my students saves all the clippings from her pet Samoyed; these long hairs can be used as is, or they can be carded and spun (see Figure 7-5). Ask your local hairdresser and dog-grooming parlor to save these for you. They should be thoroughly washed, of course, before using: make a little sack from nylon net, fill it with the hair, and tie the opening securely. Rinse the filled sack in lukewarm, sudsy water several times until the water looks clean. Rinse again in a solution of clear, warm water and about three-fourths of a cup of white vinegar. (The vinegar helps to dissipate any odors and to keep the hair soft and fluffy.) Roll in a towel and dry thoroughly.

Odds and ends of yarns are also good for stuffing. Whatever you don't use to knit your hanging can find its way into the pockets. Save all the trimmings from your projects; you will be surprised at how quickly they multiply!

Do you have an old fur coat that you no longer wear? Don't discard it — cut it up and use it. A multiple-purpose knife with a good, sharp edge, a surgeon's scalpel, or a one-sided razor blade will cut the fur easily. Work from the skin side so the hairs are left intact. If you have friends who hunt, ask them to save fur or feathers for you. Feathers, furs, and fibers, worked together in an original design, are especially handsome.

This chapter suggests only a few of the different kinds of objects that can be successfully included in knitted structures. Don't limit yourself to these examples. Like a miner searching for gold, continually be on the alert for other unusual things. Or put together ordinary objects in an extraordinary manner. Your own experiments will reveal many combinations if you keep an open mind.

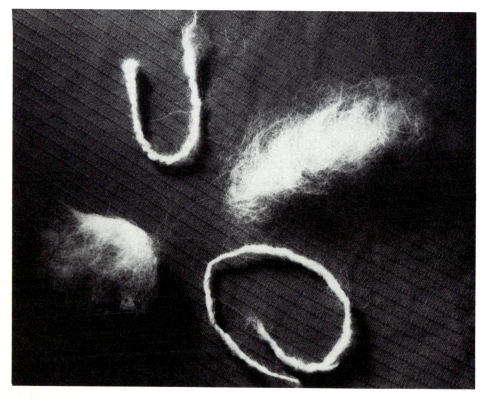

7-5. Samoyed dog hair. (Above) Carded. (Center) Raw. (Below) Spun. (Photograph by Susan Ogilvie)

8.

BUTTONS AND BEADS

Found objects lead naturally to more artificial adornments for knit art. All of us have jars or boxes filled with buttons and beads that we hope to find a use for one day; they make perfect accessories for knitted designs, since they can be incorporated in so many ways.

Do you have some insignia buttons (the ones that come on blazers)? They have strong shanks, so they can be knitted right into a hanging or sculpture (see Figure 8-1). If your button jar doesn't produce anything exciting, try secondhand or thrift shops. Yarn shops and even notions counters in department stores often sell their odd-lot buttons very cheaply to clear out their inventories. Artists who work with clay might do something special for you (see Figure 8-2).

8-1.

8-2. Hanging, knitted in cowhair, trimmed with clay beads and a bell, and mounted on ¾" doweling. Knitted by a student of Rosalie King, University of Washington. (Photograph by Mary Jane Anderson)

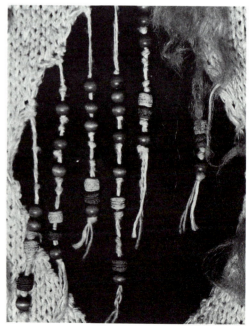

8-3 and 8-4. *Hawaii*. Hanging, knitted in wool, linen, and raw flax. Stockinette stitch, garter stitch, and bias knitting on size 11 needles. 60" long x 40" wide. (Collection of Mr. and Mrs. Denis Dwyer; photograph by Roy Goodall)

Both buttons and beads can be used to emphasize or to outline a focal point in your knit art or simply for their own pattern interest. Painted wooden beads and beads fashioned of lava rock from Hawaii were combined in the hanging shown in Figures 8-3 and 8-4. Notice that the holes are very large in order to accommodate the bulky yarn. Coral and light-brown plastic beads were arranged in a pattern to break up the solid white areas and to give more continuity to the border fringe in Figure 8-5. Multicolored plastic beads are scattered randomly in Figure C-14 so that they stand out against the relatively simple design.

Inserting beads or buttons into the fabric is a simple process: slip a loop from the left-hand needle, pull it through the hole in the bead or the shank of the button, then return it to the left-hand needle (Figure 8-6). Stretch the loop a bit so that it fits on the needle easily (be careful not to twist it), and knit it in the usual way. The bead or button may also be added after the stitch is made: slip the loop off the right-hand needle, pull it through the bead or button, then put it back on the right-hand needle (Figure 8-7). Either method is fine; the only difference is that the bead is actually knitted into the fabric in the first, whereas it is secured on the return row in the second. Beads or buttons can also be added in the purl row, and don't be afraid to insert them in the middle of a pattern stitch if you feel like it.

If the hole or shank of a bead or button is too small for the yarn you are working with, don't despair — you can sew it on later. You'll think of a sneaky way to do it, and no one will be the wiser — as long as it works!

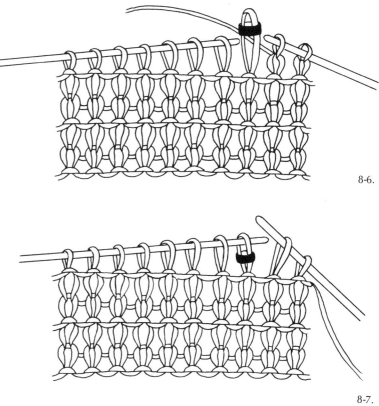

8-6.

8-7.

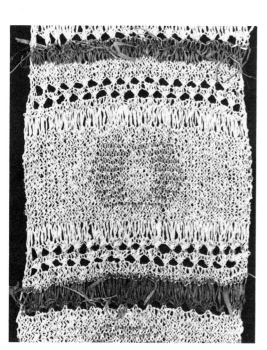

8-5. Detail of *Plastique* II (see Figure 2-26). (Photograph by Mike Sedam)

Figure 8-8 is a fine example of how beads can be used to intensify a pattern. They highlight the lacy areas, thus achieving an excellent balance. The yarn is medium-weight linen in three colors, and the beads repeat two of these.

Give serious consideration to the kinds of beads or buttons that you plan to use, particularly when your project might be handled. A fragile bead is easily broken, and there goes your design! The beads must also be light enough for your fiber or yarn; otherwise they will pull the anchor stitches out of shape. Try a sample before you begin to see what happens.

The grommets in Figures 8-9 and C-15 are obviously too heavy for the cord, but here the effect is intentional. As you become more familiar with these ways to make insertions (and no doubt invent others), you'll be able to avoid many pitfalls.

You are not restricted to buttons and beads as decorations for knit pieces. There is no limit to the number of small articles that can be successfully incorporated into a design — old costume jewelry, sequins, and little bells, to name just a few. And the possibilities become even more extensive if several of these are combined to create more complex patterns (see Figure C-16).

8-8. Hanging, knitted in off-white, light blue, and cocoa-brown linen and trimmed with white and light blue beads. Knitted by Ivarose Bovingdon. 56" long x 36" wide. (Photograph by Margaret Broughton)

8-9. Detail of *Grommets* (see Figure C-15). (Collection of Joan Hammer; photograph by Roy Goodall)

9.
TIE IT ALL UP

The finishing touches to a knit hanging or sculpture are very important: they are the mark of a carefully crafted piece of work, and they unify a design. They also provide an opportunity for your imagination to run wild — with fringing, wrapping, looping, or lacing, among other possibilities.

EDGES

FRINGING

A fringe is a very decorative edge for a hanging, and it is so easy to make. Cut a piece of cardboard about two inches wide and as long as you want the *finished* fringe to be. Either tape the cut edge of the yarn to the board or hold it down with your thumb. Wrap the yarn around the board as many times as necessary for the required amount of fringe (Figure 9-1). Cut the yarn across the top of the board. Put two, three, four, or as many strands as you like together, and fold them in half (Figure 9-2). Insert a crochet hook through a stitch wherever you wish to attach the fringe, and pull the strands through partway (Figure 9-3). Now pull the loose ends through the loop thus created (Figure 9-4).

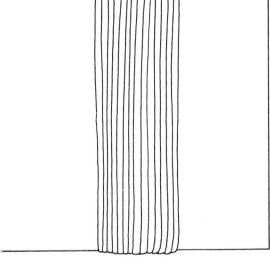

9-1.

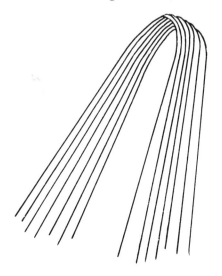

9-2.

Continue this process all along the edge you plan to fringe. To space the fringe properly, just divide the number of stitches along the edge by the number of fringes you want to attach. If the stitches are too difficult to count easily, attach a fringe at each end, and work from each side toward the middle. After all the fringes are attached, give each one an extra pull to tighten.

Figure 9-5 shows a fringe completed in this manner, and Figure 9-6 shows a variation on the basic fringe, which separates and crosses the strands, then reinforces the design with beads.

Shred the cut ends of your fringe to give it a softer appearance. Instead of leaving solid strands, separate the cut ends, and comb through them with an ordinary comb (Figure 9-7). A dog brush with firm wire bristles is great for separating the strands of some of the tougher fibers, such as sisal, jute, or rope.

Fringing on the face of the fabric is also easy to do. Select a stitch, stretch it with a crochet hook, and attach the fringe as described earlier. Figure C-17 has a profusion of individually tied strands, which were cut in eight-inch lengths, pulled through separate stitches, and tied in simple square knots. Three shades in the same color family — blue, blue-green, and green — were carefully arranged to obtain a gradual blending of the colors.

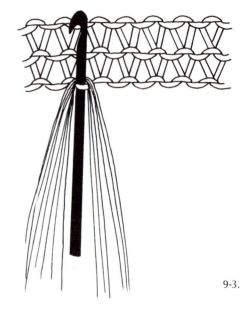

9-3.

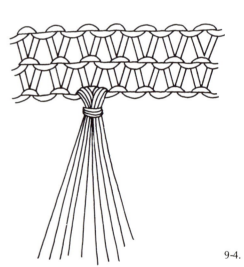

9-4.

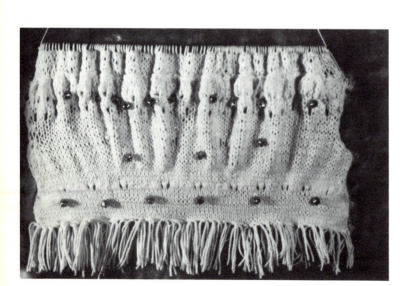

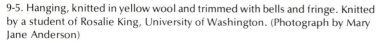

9-5. Hanging, knitted in yellow wool and trimmed with bells and fringe. Knitted by a student of Rosalie King, University of Washington. (Photograph by Mary Jane Anderson)

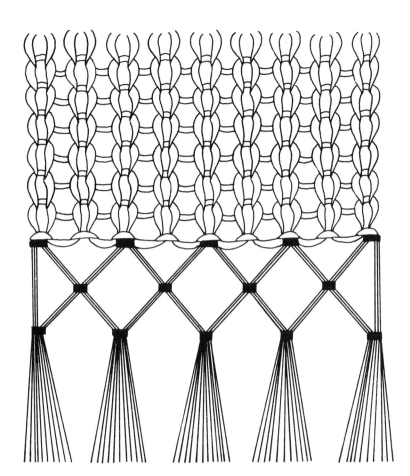

9-6.

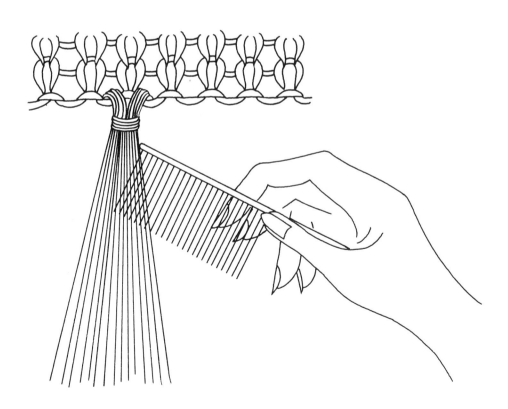

9-7.

TASSELS

Tassels are used in Figure 9-8 to accentuate the long, bellpull streamers. To make them, cut a piece of cardboard to the desired size, and wrap the yarn around and around until you have a thick bunch (Figure 9-9). Slide another piece of matching or contrasting yarn under the wrapped bunch, tie it securely on top, and cut the bunch at the bottom (Figure 9-10). About an inch or so below the top, wrap another piece of yarn around several times and tie it firmly (Figure 9-11). Trim the ends if necessary, and there's your tassel!

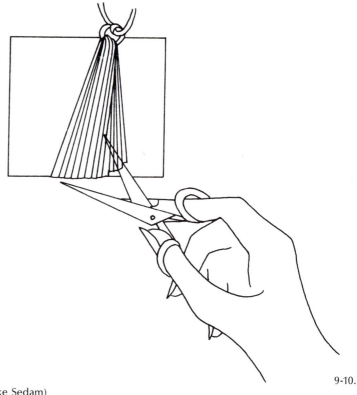

9-10.

9-8. Detail of *Caverns* (see Figure 4-5). (Photograph by Mike Sedam)

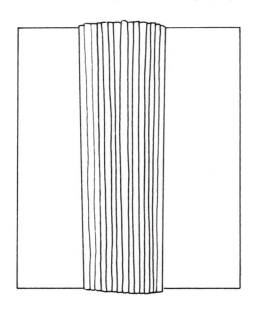

9-9.

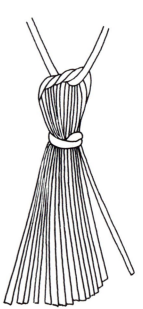

9-11.

LOOPING

The loop stitch discussed in Chapter 5 can also be used to create an interesting finish. For this purpose, the stitches are sewn rather than knitted. In Figure 9-12, the looping was done with a yarn needle and the same cord that was used in the main part of the hanging. To make a looped edge, measure a length of yarn approximately eight times the width of the hanging. Thread your yarn needle, and, starting at either edge, pull the needle up from the back and through the second stitch from the end, wrapping the yarn twice (three or four times if you prefer a larger loop) around the index finger of your left hand (Figure 9-13). Push the needle down into the first stitch, up from underneath into the second stitch, and back down into the first stitch (Figure 9-14). This makes one loop; continue in the same manner across the row. When you are finished, weave in the extra strands at the beginning and end of the row.

Loops can also be worked with a crochet hook, either for a finish or on the face of the fabric. Insert the hook into the first stitch, and wrap the thread around the second finger of your left hand (Figure 9-15). Draw through one loop, draw through two loops, take the loop off your finger, and put the hook into the next stitch (Figure 9-16). The crochet technique puts the loops on the opposite side of the fabric. If your project is free-hanging, it probably won't matter. But keep this in mind when deciding which method to use.

9-12. *Study in White*. Knitted in macramé cord and plastic twine and trimmed with glass beads. Stockinette and garter stitch on size 11 needles. 24″ long x 12″ wide. (Photograph by Roy Goodall)

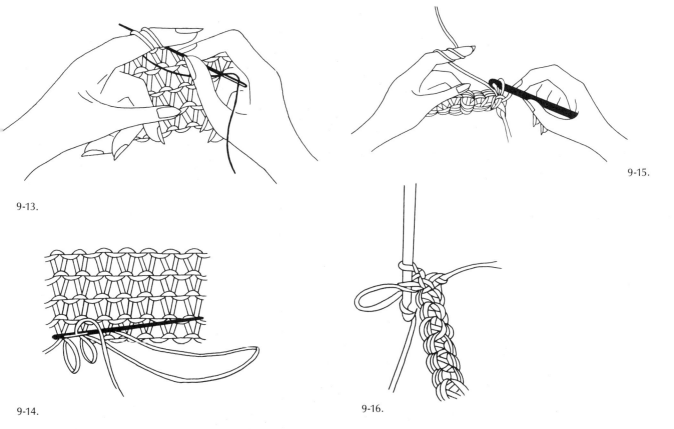

9-13.

9-15.

9-14.

9-16.

GETTING IT TOGETHER

The last step for a work of knit art is to assemble all the parts into a unified structure. The easiest join is a decorative seam. Simply whip the edges together with needle and yarn (Figure 9-17). If you want an unobtrusive seam, weave the sides together with the same yarn. Or highlight the seam with a contrasting color.

There are other occasions where a crocheted slip stitch (Figure 9-18) is the perfect solution. This makes a raised ridge, which can add still another point of interest, depending on how you integrate it into the original design.

Pliable electricians' wire, laced in and out all the way down (Figure 9-19), is still another method of joining. Just make sure that the fiber is strong enough to contain the wire, or else it will cut right through.

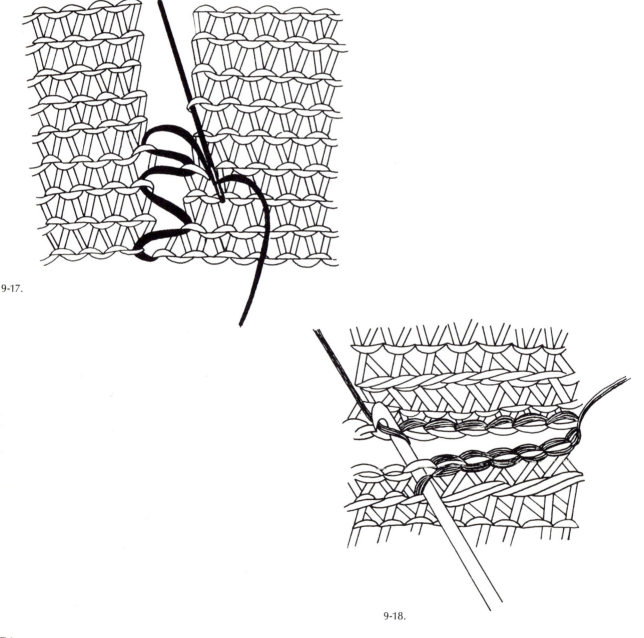

9-17.

9-18.

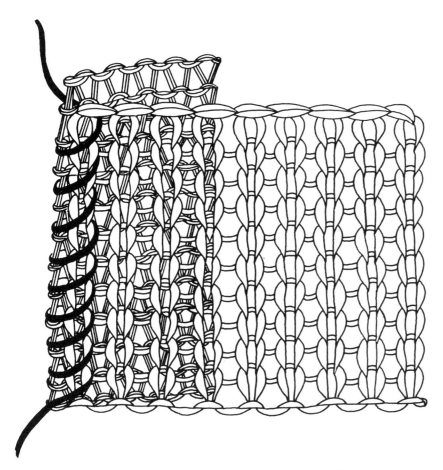

9-19.

Half-inch plastic cable is excellent for firming up circular knitting (see Figure C-10). It is strong enough to hold its shape, and it snaps right back when bent. The cable was inserted at the widest point of the round sections and whipstitched in place with matching yarn.

Wrapping is a technique in which one fiber is wrapped around a core of another fiber or some other material. It can be used to cover, to firm up an area, or to join one piece to another (see Figure 12-19). There are many methods of wrapping, such as self-cord wrapping, needle wrapping, and figure-eight wrapping, but the easiest is the following: hold the piece to be wrapped firmly in one hand and with the other hand wrap around and around this piece, carefully laying each wrap next to the previous one. From time to time, push the wraps together in order to conceal the core completely. The hula hoops in Figure C-9 were first wrapped with two strands of sisal, then joined at four strategic points by wrapping the hoops to one another. This became an important element of the structure of this free-hanging sculpture.

Almost all yarns or fibers can be wrapped. You will have to determine for yourself whether this method of joining is practical for your purposes, and your experiments will help you to decide how to use this procedure most effectively.

Think carefully about how you attach the parts of your piece together. Make up your own methods if necessary, because the joins, even if inconspicuous, are the backbone of a design.

10.

HANG IT ALL

The proper rod or hanger often makes the difference between an ordinary hanging and a truly outstanding one. While you are working, think about how and where your piece will be displayed. Keep your eyes open for just the right thing to hang it from. The kinds of hangers are as varied as the kinds of fibers. An interesting or unusual hanger like a piece of driftwood (see Figures 10-1 and 10-2), a pair of garden shears (see Figure C-18), or a clothes hanger (see Figure 10-3) might set the tone; on the other hand, so much may be happening in the hanging itself that an obtrusive hanger would spoil the whole effect.

A clear Plexiglas rod provides an efficient means of display without detracting from the hanging (see Figure 10-4). A commercial plastics company will make this kind of rod to your exact requirements. Plexiglas is available in diameters ranging from one-eighth inch (used in Figure 6-2) to three inches, or you can buy an eight-foot length, cut it, and mold it to any shape by heating it carefully in a low oven.

Then there is that old standby, wooden doweling (see Figure 10-5). It is easily tailored to fit your particular purpose, down to the tiny size that was used to hang Figure C-19, and you can paint it, stain it, shellac it, or even wrap your fiber around it.

If you want to enclose your project within the limits of a frame, half-round baseboard molding, another household material, is easily fashioned into one. The molding in Figure 10-6 was cut in four sixty-six-inch lengths, painted black, then fitted together to make a collapsible frame. (My husband designed this frame so that it could be easily dismantled for shipping.) The jute was threaded through loop screws affixed approximately two inches apart along the top and bottom in order to stretch the fabric taut.

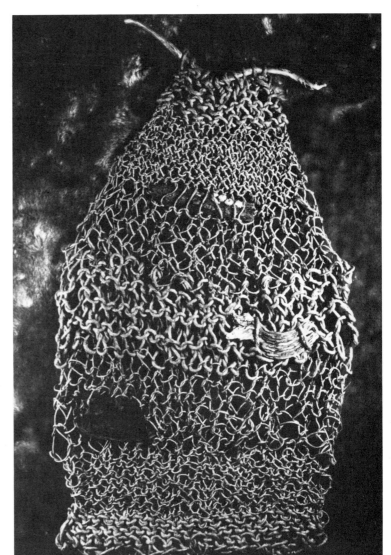

10-1. Hanging, knitted in two weights of twine and mounted on driftwood. Knitted by a student of Rosalie King, University of Washington. (Photograph by Mary Jane Anderson)

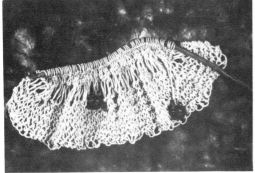

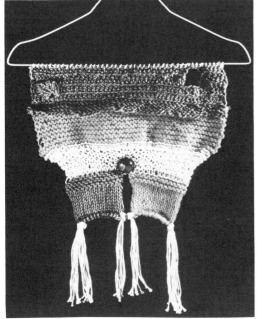

10-2. Yarn sculpture, knitted free-form in ecru yarn, mounted on driftwood, and trimmed with old sleigh bells. Knitted by a student of Rosalie King, University of Washington. (Photograph by Mary Jane Anderson)

10-3. Hanging, knitted in red, brown, and white wool, trimmed with a brooch, and mounted on a clothes hanger, which functions as part of the design. Knitted by a student of Rosalie King, University of Washington. (Photograph by Mary Jane Anderson)

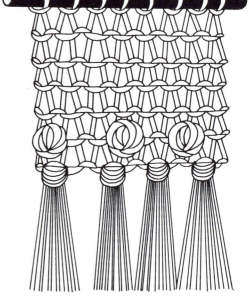

10-5.

10-4. *Owl*. Hanging, knitted in rygja wool and cotton twine, decorated with fringe and tiny bells, and mounted on a Plexiglas rod. 72″ long x 48″ wide. (Photograph by Mike Sedam)

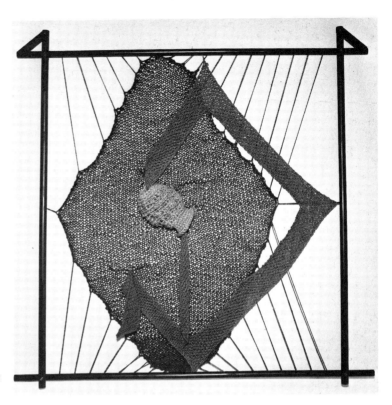

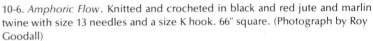

10-6. *Amphoric Flow*. Knitted and crocheted in black and red jute and marlin twine with size 13 needles and a size K hook. 66" square. (Photograph by Roy Goodall)

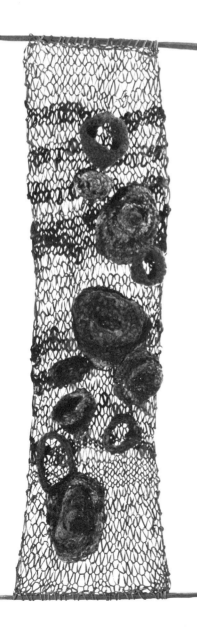

Ethnic shops featuring artifacts from countries around the world are great treasure houses of unusual woods, such as myrtle and teak, and metal pieces, such as swords or medallions, that can be adapted to a fiber hanging. Also look for these when you travel. Some of the most interesting findings in my stowaway cabinet were discovered in little shops tucked away in back alleys and untouristy side streets.

Again, your own woodpile may provide you with all you need. Slender strips of kindling can be stained and used to make firm top and bottom rods. The rods in Figure 10-7 appear to blend completely into the natural colors of the hanging.

Remember that your hanger must not only suit your design but also the fabric itself. Homespun wool, for example, is much too soft to hang freely from a conventional rod or disk. The most satisfactory solution for this material as used in this design was to mount it on plywood cut to the exact shape of the design (see Figure 2-20). For this procedure, paint the wood an appropriate color, then fasten the fabric to the plywood with slightly diluted white glue.

10-7. *Earth*. Hanging, knitted and crocheted in leather lacing and handspun wool. Stockinette stitch and garter stitch on sizes 11 and 15 needles. 48" long x 18" wide. (Photograph by Mike Sedam)

CASING

A casing is a durable enclosure for a rod or hanger. It can also be a specific element of a design. There are three satisfactory ways to make a casing: (1) it can be knitted in along with your work, (2) folded over and sewn in later, or (3) knitted separately and sewn to the backside of your work.

1. To knit the casing, leave all the stitches on the needle, and turn the reverse side of the fabric toward you. Measure the circumference of the rod, and fold over toward the right side as many rows as are needed to accommodate it (Figure 10-8). Holding your work in a knitting position (stitches on the left-hand needle), insert the right-hand needle into the back of the first stitch on the left-hand needle, pick up a loop from the work directly behind that stitch, and knit both together (Figure 10-9). Knit across the row in this manner until all the stitches on the left-hand needle are worked (Figure 10-10). Make sure that all the loops picked up from the fabric are on the same row. (It might be helpful to weave a strand of different-colored yarn across the loops to be picked up; it can easily be removed after you finish.) If you want the casing to show on the face of your work (see Figure 10-11), reverse the process.

2. To sew the casing after your work is finished, take up a fold, baste along the base of the fold with a blunt-point yarn needle threaded with a contrasting color of yarn, then sew along this same edge with ordinary back stitch. If you have a good eye, you probably won't need to baste; it simply helps to keep the fold even.

3. For a sew-on casing, cast on the same number of stitches as in your hanging, and work in stockinette or garter stitch as many rows as necessary for the circumference of your rod. Bind off loosely, and sew this band to the back of your hanging.

You will spend as much time trying to decide how to hang your design as you do knitting it, but the extra time is well worth it. There is a deep satisfaction when the rod or frame, the design, and the fibers all come together (see Figure 10-12). These few suggestions are meant only to spur your own fantasies, so dream on.

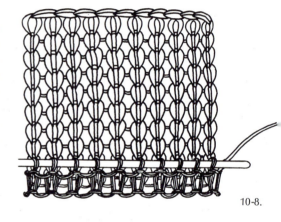

10-8.

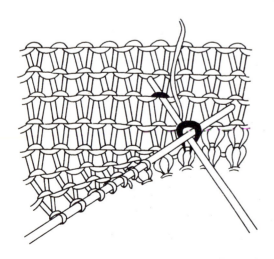

10-9.

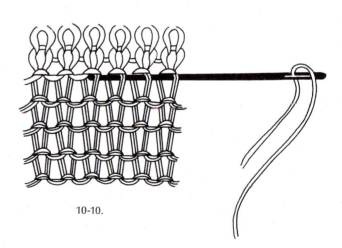

10-10.

10-11.

10-12. *Viscera*. Knitted and crocheted in sailor's twelve-ply rope, natural linen, jute, and handspun wool and mounted on black vinyl. 36" long x 24" wide. (Photograph by Roy Goodall)

11.

FASHION-WISE

Casting on, binding off, increasing and decreasing, and elongating stitches are actually fashion techniques adapted to a distinctive art form. It's only fair to transfer this art form back to contemporary fashion and see what results.

Fashion designers have finally recognized the marvelous durability and originality of handknit garments. Both wools and synthetics are now machine-washable, and most are mothproofed. As for design — anything goes! Only a few years ago a handknitted two-piece swimsuit garnered some raised eyebrows, and handknitted pants were unthinkable. But today the pattern books are filled with directions on how to knit swimsuits, beach cover-ups, evening gowns, and pants that look as good, feel as good, and perhaps fit better than some machine-knit and woven materials. The following are just a few examples of what can be done by applying a free-form approach to handknitted clothing.

A long skirt is a staple in most wardrobes today, and what could be more elegant than the lovely wool version shown in Figure 11-1? Basic stockinette stitch was used for the main part of the skirt, and yellow squares knitted in a regular pattern sequence contrast with blue and white crocheted areas to provide the border interest.

Halters are also very popular nowadays. Figure 11-2 shows a version in linen, which features simple knitting and crocheting. Two kinds of beads and a fringe serve as texture contrasts, and a handmade ceramic medallion provides the focal point.

The spectacular shawl shown in Figure 11-3 also combined basic knitting and crochet techniques. Tassels and fringes were added to natural wools in different weights, naps, and colors to create a provocative interplay of surface textures.

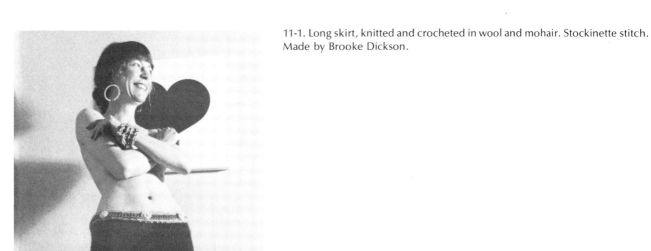

11-1. Long skirt, knitted and crocheted in wool and mohair. Stockinette stitch. Made by Brooke Dickson.

11-2. Halter, knitted and crocheted in natural linen and trimmed with a ceramic medallion, Hebron glass beads, and ceramic beads. (Photograph by Ray Kaltenbach)

11-3. Shawl, knitted and crocheted in gray, brown, and wine wool and mohair. Made by Brooke Dickson.

Another lovely shawl is shown in Figure C-20. Garter stitch was used for the main part, then a macramé fringe was attached to a double-crochet border. The combination of these three companion crafts sets off the beauty of the light, frothy mohair yarn. The strong green makes a definite visual impact, so additional color embellishments were unnecessary.

Knit-art techniques can rejuvenate your outdated wearables. An old dress is transformed by a knit border of several colors, one of which matches or blends with the color of the dress; a lush fringe gives the same dress an instant contemporary look.

A multicolored or profusely trimmed sweater, vest, or jacket can be worn with almost anything. Appliqué knitted squares in different colors on a basic sweater, or use a glossy metallic. Insert beads or paillettes — there's no end to the possibilities. Leftover black synthetic yarn and odds and ends of silver and gold brocade were knitted together in the evening sweater shown in Figure 11-4, and gold brocade alone forms the unusual loincloth in Figure C-21. Both are beautiful to wear over a skirt or pants. Accessories like these are outrageously expensive in boutiques or specialty shops but cost almost nothing when you make them yourself from what you have lying around. Better yet, you have a truly one-of-a-kind garment.

For chilly winter days, what could be more practical than a handknitted stocking hat? Because the elegant handspun wool in Figure 11-5 gives such a rich texture, only a simple stockinette stitch was used.

11-4. Evening sweater, knitted in gold and silver brocade and black Orlon. Stockinette stitch on size 9 needles. (Photograph by Roy Goodall)

11-5. Stocking hat, knitted in multicolored handspun wool. Made by Paula Simmons. (Photograph by Ross Simmons)

84

The wise designer kept to basic knitting and crocheting techniques in fashioning the unusual dress of lavender and white wool shown in Figure 11-6. The dramatic combination of colors is the important element here.

Ribbons and gathers (see Chapter 2) can be amusing in handknit garments. The excess weight can be uncomfortable, however, so you should use a fine yarn. Knit garments, particularly long ones for evening, should move easily with the natural movement of the body. Don't overembellish your clothing; my years of designing experience have convinced me that understatement is more elegant than overstatement, and none of the excitement of original design is lost in the process. You can worry a design to pieces, thereby defeating its impact and fashion value.

Let's not exclude men from the fashion world. It is refreshing to see them becoming more aware of design and more free in their use of color. Many knit-design ideas can be adapted to men's clothing: a handsome shirt with a leather-and-yarn fringe, for example, or a caftan for relaxing at home. Figures C-22 and C-23 show an elementary design consisting of four rectangular pieces in two shades of purple that were knitted in stockinette stitch with size 9 needles. The side seams were left open for about twelve inches from the shoulder seams to form the armholes. The front seam was started eight inches below the top to make a V neckline, and the shoulder seams were closed to within four inches on either side of the neck opening. The multicolored crocheted borders and the appliquéd sphere on the back were added after the caftan was assembled. A narrow, bias-knitted strip was attached to the inside as a facing to firm up the neckline. (An eight- or ten-stitch strip is wide enough for this purpose.) For a little more pizzazz, you might add patch pockets with the same multicolored trim.

The caftan can also be knitted in eight separate sections, alternating the colors: just divide each rectangle in half, and sew the sections together checkerboard fashion.

This fundamental design is equally suitable for women and easily adjusted to fit children. Worn over a turtleneck sweater or a body suit, it's just right for winter evenings and perfect for après-ski. Consider the uncluttered fabric as a canvas for your own ingenuity, an opportunity to create clothing art!

The men of tropical countries have been wearing multicolored, knitted clothing for a long time. This coca bag (Figure 11-7, left) is knitted with many colors of handspun wool on very tiny, circular needles. The man's shoulder bag (Figure 11-7, right) is an example of two-color knitting in a more conservative pattern. It is also knitted on very small needles.

11-6. Dress, knitted and crocheted in lavender and white wool. Made by Brooke Dickson.

11-7. (Left) Coca bag from Cochabamba, Bolivia, knitted in handspun sheep's wool. This bag is used for carrying coca leaves; small pouches on the sides hold limes. (Right) Man's shoulder bag from Solala, Guatemala, knitted in brown and beige handspun wool with a woven strap. (Collection of the Costume and Textile Study Center, School of Home Economics, University of Washington; photograph by Mary Jane Anderson)

FITTING CLOTHES

There is one catch when knit-art techniques are applied to garments: the stitch gauge must be measured carefully to ensure an accurate fit. This is quite contradictory to what I've said in earlier chapters, but where clothing is involved, proper fit is just as important as original design. A little carelessness, however, is easily remedied.

It was only because I hated the look of skirts knitted on circular needles (they clung so unattractively and did not drape well) that I learned how to cut handknitted material. After many months of searching for a dress pattern knitted in separate pieces, I finally found a French one that was exactly what I had been looking for. It was beautifully designed, with elegant lines and dressmaker detailing, and charted for a size 1 needle with very fine dress yarn. The pattern was in French, of course, so I sat hour after hour with the pattern on one side and a French-English dictionary on the other, patiently wading my way through every word. When I was finished and held up the pieces to have some idea of how they would go together, I wanted to cry — they were miles too big! A whole year's work down the drain! What I had neglected to take into account was that European measurements were gauged by the metric table, so my dress was two-and-a-half sizes too large. I just couldn't bear the thought of ripping out all those pieces, and that's when I became brave enough to cut them — to treat them like woven material. It was a most traumatic experience, but as I became more familiar with the technique, I discovered how practical it was to simply cut the pattern pieces to fit, taking into account the fiber content of the yarn. If you sew, apply this knowledge to your knitting needles. I think you'll be happy with the results.

If your garment is too big, take it in with an ordinary dressmaker seam (Figure 11-8), handling the material like a woven fabric. If you make a mistake in charting, don't rip out all those stitches; just stitch up the seam on the sewing machine. This makes a very neat seam, but use the longest stitch, and pull the material slightly to allow for some elasticity and to keep the stitches from popping.

If your garment is much too big and there is a lot of extra material, cut it! After you stitch the seam, make another double row of stitching about five-eighths inch further out on each side of the open seam, then cut between these two rows of stitching (Figure 11-9). When you finish, open up the seam, and press it down lightly with a steam iron.

If you are using wool yarn and your garment is too small, you can block it out with the iron, because the steam relaxes the fibers. Wool is so elastic that you can anticipate approximately one to one-and-a-half inches of stretch: when you are planning your garment, cast on fewer stitches than you think you will need. For instance, if your gauge is five stitches to the inch and you want your finished material to measure twenty inches across, cast on ninety-two stitches instead of one hundred stitches. The garment can then be blocked out to the required measurement.

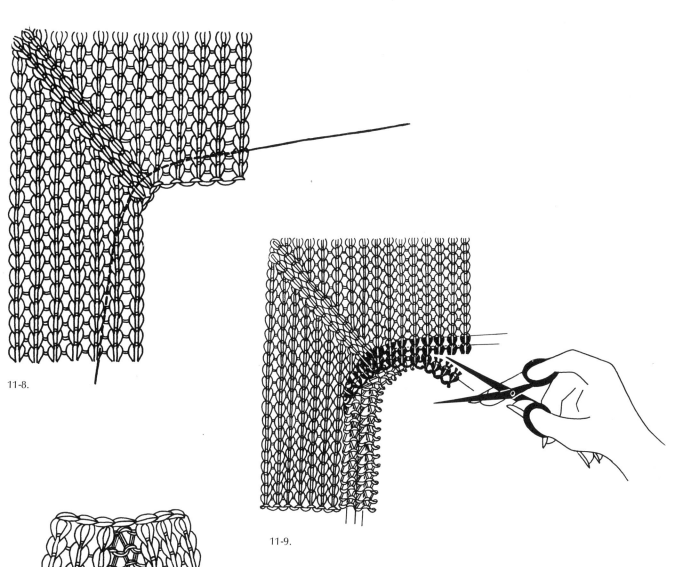

11-8.

11-9.

11-10.

Linen, cotton, synthetics, and synthetic blends, on the other hand, must be knit to fit exactly. It's all right to press linen or cotton lightly for a more finished look, but *never, never* use heat on synthetics. If you miscalculate and your garment is too small, knit a gusset (Figure 11-10) to insert at the sides between the front and back and into the sleeves if necessary. (I call this an architectural adjustment.) For variety, the gusset can be knitted in a contrasting color that is carried out in another part of the garment.

The creative possibilities of knit art in fashion are vast. Interesting color combinations, free-form crocheted embellishments, some strategically placed buttons or beads, and one or two basic knitting techniques (used singly or in combination) are all you need to make a personal statement, and how original you'll be!

12.

SIMPLE CROCHET

Many of the examples of knit art shown on these pages incorporate the companion craft of crochet. Beautiful designs can be produced by combining the two crafts, and a discussion of some of the basic techniques of crochet is especially appropriate in this book, because it has been accepted as an art form for several years. All you need are a couple of crochet hooks and some yarn. If you've never crocheted, practice the mechanics of holding the crochet hook and working with the yarn until you become comfortable with them.

CROCHET STITCHES

CHAIN STITCH

Chain stitch is the foundation for all the other stitches of crochet. First, make a loop (Figure 12-1). Pass the hook through this loop to the left side of your yarn and underneath, catch the yarn, and draw it through the loop (Figure 12-2). Continue in this way to make a chain of whatever length you wish. To make a circular form, crochet a chain of six or eight loops, and join the starting and end loops of the chain with a slip stitch (Figure 12-3).

SINGLE CROCHET STITCH

To make a *single crochet stitch*, skip the first chain stitch, and slip the hook into the next chain. Pass the yarn around the hook as described above, and draw the loop through the two loops on the hook (Figure 12-4).

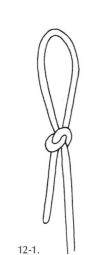

12-1.

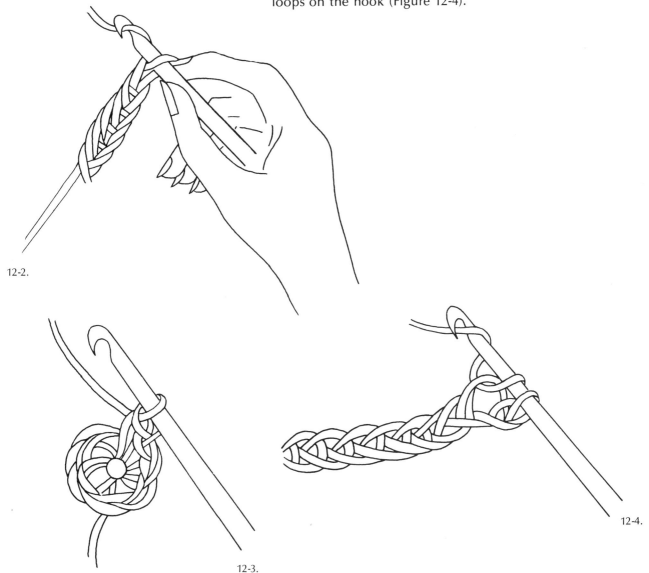

12-2.

12-3.

12-4.

DOUBLE CROCHET STITCH

To make a *double crochet stitch*, skip the first two chains, wrap the yarn around the hook, and insert the hook into the third chain, catching the yarn. Draw the yarn through and onto the hook. Now catch the yarn again, and draw it through the first two loops. Catch it again, and pull it through the two loops (Figure 12-5).

To increase single or double crochet stitch, simply work two stitches in one stitch. Increasing in every link in the chain obviously doubles the number of stitches, causing the work to ruffle, so it is wise to work the increases on every other row. You may, however, *want* this effect. For a more gradual enlargement, space out the increases in every second or third stitch. Experiment until you have some idea of how it works.

Skip a stitch and work the next stitch to decrease single (Figure 12-6) or double (Figure 12-7) crochet stitch.

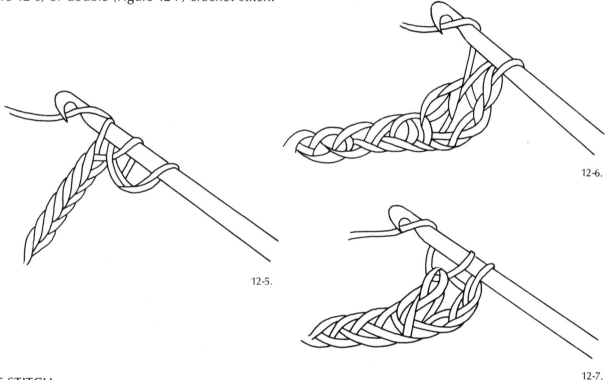

12-6.

12-5.

12-7.

FILET STITCH

If the vertical slits between double crochet stitches are enlarged by spacing the stitches, a mesh (usually square) is created that is called *filet stitch* (see Figure 12-18). The spacing is controlled by adding one or more chains between stitches and skipping a corresponding number on the previous row.

PINEAPPLE STITCH

The *pineapple stitch* (see Figure C-21) is one version of a compound or clustered stitch. It is made from a foundation chain. Wrap the hook, insert it into the fifth chain, and draw out a long loop (the length of three or four chain stitches). Repeat this procedure four times. Catch the yarn and draw it through all but two of the loops on the hook. Catch the yarn again and draw it through the remaining loops to lock the stitch.

CROCHETED SOFT JEWELRY

Continuing the fashion theme of the previous chapter, beautiful pieces of jewelry are used to illustrate some of the possibilities of simple crochet stitches, either alone or in combination with knitting techniques. Their size makes it easier to see the effect of the stitches on the total design, but remember that crochet art, like knit art, is unlimited in scope — use it to construct anything at all that suits your fancy!

The sculpture shown in Figures 12-8 and C-24 is really a spoof. It is worked with opaque, white plastic wrapping twine and is both knitted and crocheted in alternately irregular sections, with crocheted ruffles defining those areas. After the tube was completed, it was stuffed with several hundred plastic vegetable bags. The smaller forms at the base, all done in single crochet in brown, charcoal, black, and blue metallic yarns, were stitched on later. It is seventy inches long.

12-8. Detail of *Celia's Jools* (see Figure C-24). Photograph by Roy Goodall)

The raccoon-skin pendant (Figure 12-9) is backed by charcoal-brown handspun wool that is single crocheted to the natural shape of the fur and trimmed with glass beads for the eyes and nose. It is hung from a chain of the same wool with bright-colored beads inserted in a consistent pattern through the chain. The dangling metal pieces are attached by wrapping (see Chapter 9).

Mottled blue and brown, handcrafted stone beads crocheted directly into the fabric with single crochet provide unusual textural contrast with the brown lamé yarn in Figure 12-10. Two slender, wrapped fringes add a delicate finishing touch.

Body jewelry reminiscent of ancient times is being worn more and more. The bib shown in Figures 12-11 and 12-12 is constructed of solid circular areas of single crochet interconnected by floating strands of crocheted chains. The gold metallic yarn is a washable synthetic.

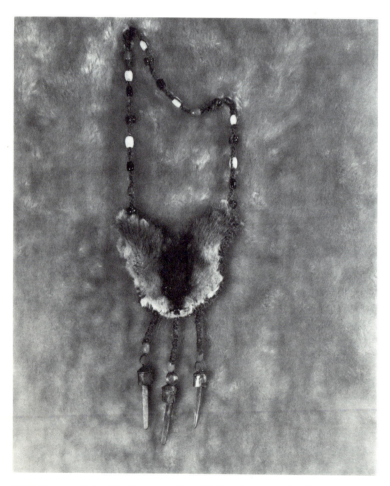

12-9. *Raccoon Baby*. Necklace, crocheted in handspun wool and trimmed with fur, bones, metal, and glass beads. (Photograph by Mary Jane Anderson)

12-10. *Amorphous*. Necklace, crocheted in brown lamé and trimmed with stone beads. (Photograph by Mary Jane Anderson)

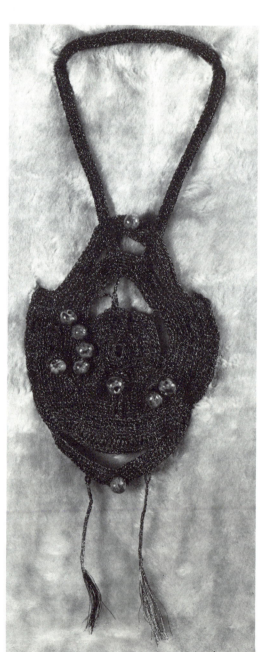

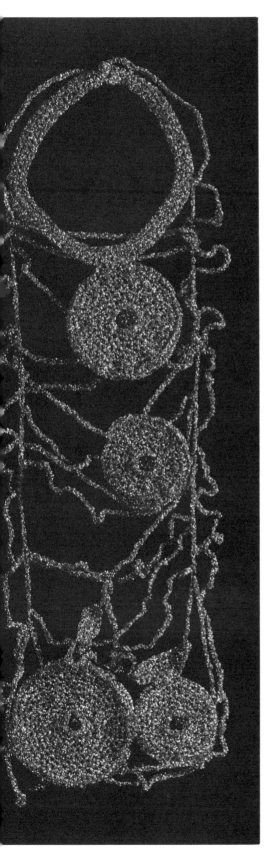

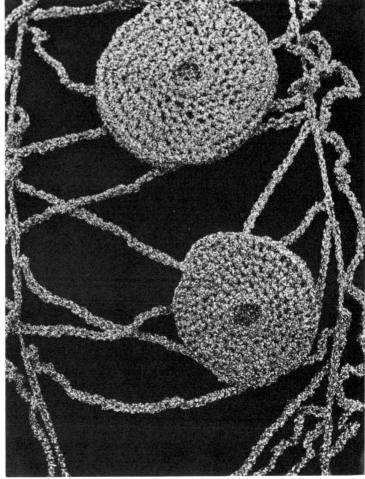

12-11 and 12-12. *Medallions*. Bib, crocheted in gold metallic yarn. Single crochet stitch. (Photographs by Mary Jane Anderson and Roy Goodall)

Figure 12-13 shows a series of tubular forms attached in regular sequences around the perimeter of the collar of this silver brocade neckpiece, again demonstrating the flexibility of a single crochet stitch.

Figure 12-14 demonstrates how tubular forms affixed to a flat surface can create a three-dimensional effect. Single, double, pineapple, and filet crochet sections radiate out from the center, with hand-painted wooden beads for emphasis. The materials are woolen rug yarn, cotton string, and linen.

The medallion in Figure 12-15 is crocheted with double strands of charcoal and silver metallic yarn in single crochet and crisscrossed with taughtly stretched chains, which give a shadowy effect. The disk is suspended from a tube made by folding a flat piece in half and slip stitching the edges together. The dull black lava-rock beads are laced onto the fringes.

12-13. *Barrels*. Necklace, crocheted in silver brocade. Single crochet stitch. (Collection of Mrs. Arthur Nusbaum; photograph by Mary Jane Anderson)

12-14. *Motif 2*. Bib, crocheted in multicolored cotton and rayon and trimmed with multicolored beads. Single, double, pineapple, and filet stitch. (Photograph by Roy Goodall)

12-15. *Volcano*. Bib, crocheted in charcoal metallic thread and trimmed with black lava-rock beads. Single crochet stitch. (Photo by Mary Jane Anderson)

The focal point of the gold brocade collar in Figure 12-16 is a window-shade pull covered by single crochet. The double-layered circular sections, made by increasing and decreasing, as described earlier, are connected by chains.

Leftover lengths of wool, linen, and rayon yarns are combined in the body piece shown in Figure 12-17. Crocheted loop stitching defines the interior areas. The colors are orange and two shades of green.

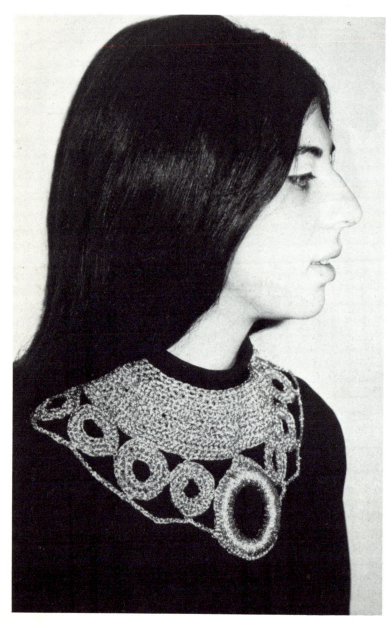

12-16. *Nefertiti*. Collar, crocheted in gold brocade and trimmed with a covered window-shade pull. (Modeled by Wendy Cone)

12-17. *Motif 3*. Bib, crocheted in multicolored wool, linen, and rayon. Single, double, pineapple, and filet stitch. (Photograph by Mary Jane Anderson)

The fiber in Figure 12-18 is of prime interest. Double strands of fake suede in double crochet stitch form the two-sided pendant. Free-hanging chains spill from the surface. The collar is formed by open filet areas separated by rows of double crochet. This material has the added advantages of being washable and quick-drying. The colors are lime green and pink.

The elegant evening bag (Figure 12-19) is heightened by fur trimming. Four separate ovals of double-stranded silver brocade crocheted in single stitch were slip stitched together, then lined with China silk. The silver-fox tails were first wrapped and then sewn to the underside of the bag.

Fake suede is used again in Figure 12-20 to fashion a vestment. Yellow feathers were individually wrapped and attached along the vertical strips. Mottled brown and yellow feathers were then sewn around the neckpiece, and light-brown plastic beads were fastened at the juncture points.

12-18. *Squiggles*. Neckpiece, crocheted in pink, purple, and lime fake suede. Single and filet stitch. (Photograph by Mary Jane Anderson)

12-19. Evening bag, crocheted in silver brocade, trimmed with silver-fox tails, and lined in China silk. (Photograph by Roy Goodall)

12-20. Vestment, crocheted in yellow fake suede and trimmed with feathers.
(Photograph by Roy Goodall)

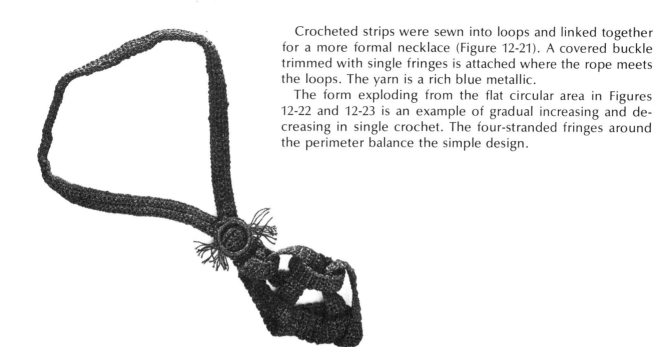

Crocheted strips were sewn into loops and linked together for a more formal necklace (Figure 12-21). A covered buckle trimmed with single fringes is attached where the rope meets the loops. The yarn is a rich blue metallic.

The form exploding from the flat circular area in Figures 12-22 and 12-23 is an example of gradual increasing and decreasing in single crochet. The four-stranded fringes around the perimeter balance the simple design.

12-21. *Jigsaw*. Neckpiece, crocheted in electric blue metallic yarn. Single crochet stitch. (Collection of Mrs. Gerald Cone; photograph by Roy Goodall)

12-22 and 12-23. *Secrets*. Necklace, crocheted in gold brocade. Single crochet stitch. (Collection of Mrs. R. Keith Cameron; photograph by Mary Jane Anderson)

A simple rope (Figure 12-24), ending in bulbous forms with single strands of fringe, can be worn either around the waist or twisted at the neck. A matching wristlet has the same bulbous form floating from an oval space created by dividing the piece in half and crocheting back and forth on each side with separate balls of yarn.

Shoulder bags are truly high fashion. Figure 12-25 shows a bag of black lamé twisted with bronze metallic yarn and worked into a simple square. A pocket was attached to the back of the bag to hold small change and a handkerchief, and crystal beads highlight the turned-back edges. The same yarn was used in Figure C-25 to fashion a hip-hugging belt of crossed loops of chains with irregularly shaped forms attached randomly.

All of the foregoing examples in this chapter have one thing in common — elementary stitches were used to make many different kinds of shapes and forms. These simple techniques, used creatively and spontaneously with exotic yarns and fibers, can produce articles of great beauty.

Jewelry is a craft in which novel and innovative designs have frequently been developed, and which perhaps brings knitting or crocheting closest to what is traditionally thought of as art. But my intention throughout this book was to present in a simple, direct way some unfamiliar alternatives to conventional knitting: to exaggerate shapes, to insert found objects, to create exciting forms; in other words, to consider knitting as a true art form rather than merely a utilitarian craft. I hope that your own creativity will now encourage you to experiment far beyond these suggestions. Whether you have been knitting for a long time or are just becoming acquainted with the craft, if I have stimulated your imagination even a tiny bit, this book will have served its purpose well. Just imagine knit — it will happen! Happy knitting.

12-24. Rope and wristlet, crocheted in gold brocade. Single crochet stitch.

12-25. *Mad Money*. Shoulder bag, crocheted in lamé and metallic yarn and trimmed with crystal beads. Single crochet stitch. (Photograph by Mary Jane Anderson)

BIBLIOGRAPHY

Knitting Dictionary (Mon Tricot). Crown Publishers, New York, 1971.

MacKenzie, Clinton D. *New Design in Crochet.* Van Nostrand Reinhold Company, New York, 1972.

Meilach, Dona Z. *Creating Art from Fibers and Fabrics*. Henry Regnery Company, Chicago, 1972.

Phillips, Mary Walker. *Creative Knitting*. Van Nostrand Reinhold Company, New York, 1971.

Rainey, Sarita R. *Weaving Without a Loom*. Davis Publications, Worcester, 1966.

Thomas, Mary. *Mary Thomas's Knitting Book.* Hodder and Stoughton, Ltd., London, 1938.

Walker, Barbara G. *The Craft of Lace Knitting*. Charles Scribner's Sons, New York, 1971.

————. *A Treasury of Knitting Patterns.* Charles Scribner's Sons, New York, 1968.

Wilson, Jean. *Weaving You Can Wear*. Van Nostrand Reinhold Company, New York, 1973.

————. *Weaving is Fun*. Van Nostrand Reinhold Company, New York, 1971.

SUPPLIERS

RETAIL:
Cottage Crafts, Pomfret Center, Conn. 06259

Craft Yarns of Rhode Island, Inc., P.O. Box 385, Pawtucket, R.I. 02862

Creative Handweavers, P.O. Box 26480, Los Angeles, Calif. 90026

Earthworks, 624 W. Willow, Chicago, Ill. 60614

Handcraft House, 110 West Esplanade, North Vancouver, B.C.

Nature's Fibers, 109 Tinker Street, Woodstock, N.Y. 12498

Potomac Yarn Products Company, P.O. Box 2367, Dept. 1A, Chapel Hill, N.C. 27514

WHOLESALE: MANUFACTURERS OF QUALITY DOMESTIC YARNS:
Bear Brand Yarns, 230 Fifth Avenue, New York, N.Y. 10001
Spinnerin Yarn Co., Inc., 230 Fifth Avenue, New York, N.Y. 10001

INDEX

Abbreviations of knitting terms 20
Amounts of material, estimating 47
Appliqué 39, 84, 85

Bag, coca 85; evening 97;
    shoulder 85, 100
Beads 58, 65-68, 82, 94, 97, 100
Bells 68
Belt 100
Bias knitting 28-29, 34, 58, 85
Bib 92
Binding off 26-27
Blocking 86
Body jewelry 92
Brocade yarn 84, 94, 96, 97
Buttons 39, 65-68

Cable needle 53
Cable stitch 56
Caftan 85
Casings 58, 80
Casting on 26-27
Cat's Eye stitch 55
Chain stitch 89
Changing direction in knitting 32
Circular knitting 32-33
Circular needles 18-19, 32-33, 50, 85
Clothes hanger 76
Clothing 82-87
Cluster stitch 90
Color 36-39
Combining yarns 42, 57
Cords 40, 47
Cotton 19, 25, 34, 40, 42; pressing 87;
    testing 45
Cowhair 42
Crochet 57, 74, 84, 88-100; hook, for
    fringe 69-70; for loops 73; sizes 19
Crossed insertion 53
Cross-stitch cable 56
Curtain stretcher 45
Cutting board 45, 46
Cutting knits 86

Decreasing, crochet 90, 96, 99;
    knitting 22-23
Diamonds 23
Discards 61, 63
Dog hair 64
Double crochet stitch 90, 94, 97
Double knitting 63
Double-pointed needle 32, 33, 53

Doweling 76
Draping 25
Dress 85
Dress yarns 40
Dried objects 61
Driftwood 61, 63, 76
Dry-cleanability 61
Dye lots 47

Edges 69-73
Embroidery 39, 57
Enlarging garments 86
Estimating amounts of material 47
Evening sweater 84

Fake suede 97
Feathers 64, 97
Fibers 40-47; blends 19, 25; natural 19;
    synthetic 19
Filet stitch 90, 94, 97
Finishing 69-75
Firming knits 45-47
Fitting clothes 86
Flax 19
Found objects 61-64
Fox tails 97
Fringe 34, 58, 69-70, 82, 92, 94, 99, 100
Fur 64, 97

Garter stitch 20
Goat hair 42
Grand eyelet lace 34, 54
Greek key 26
Grommets 68
Gusset 87

Half-round molding 76
Halter 82
Hau fiber 40, 47
Holes 30-31
Homespun wool 42, 47, 57, 84
Hoops, wrapped 75
Horsehair 42
Human hair 42

Increasing; crochet 90, 96, 99;
    knitting 22-33
Indian cross-stitch 53

Jewelry, crochet 91-100
Jute 19, 25, 34, 36, 45, 47, 63, 70

Knitting terms 20
Knitting-worsted 40
Lamé 100
Leather 25, 34, 40, 46, 57
Leftovers 42-44, 96
Linen 25, 34, 42, 87, 96; pressing 87; testing 45
Loincloth 84
Long needles 50
Long skirt 82
Looping 73
Loop screws 76
Loop stitch, crochet 96; knitting 49

Machine sewing knits 86
Macramé 84
Make-a-Shade 46
Markers 19, 32, 63
Materials 19, 40-47
Medallion 79, 82, 94
Metallic yarn 19, 91-96, 99, 100
Mock cable rib 56
Mohair 84
Moss stitch 54

Nails 61
Necklace 99
Needles, aluminum 18; cable 53; circular 18-19, 32-33, 50, 85; double-pointed 33; doweling 18; kit 18-19; length 18-19; plastic 18; size, 18-19, 22, 27; straight 33; wooden 18; yarn 19, 80
Novelty yarns 19

Openings 30-31; diamond 28; triangle 28
Overlay 39

Paper fiber 19
Pattern stitches 48-56
Pineapple stitch 90, 94
Plexiglas 58, 76
Plywood mounting 79
Pockets 58, 63-64, 100
Popcorn stitch 55, 58
Purl stitch 20
Purse stitch 49

Raffia 19, 47
Rayon 36, 47, 96
Rectangles 34
Recycling 44, 61, 64
Ribbons 22, 58, 85
Ribbon yarn 19
Rigidity 46
Rocks 58, 61, 63
Rope 47, 61, 70
Rubber hose 19
Rug wool 58

Satin 39
Screws 76
Seams 33, 74
Seaweed 61
Seed stitch 54
Sequins 68
Sewing knits 33, 74
Sewn looping 73

Shade pull 96
Shaping 22-35
Shawl 84
Shells 61, 63
Short rows 25
Shoulder bag 85, 100
Shredding fringe 70
Silk 19, 47
Single crochet stitch 89, 94, 96
Sisal 19, 42, 70
Skirt 82
Slip stitch 89
Slits 31
Slub yarn 19
Square knots 70
Squares 34
Starching 45
Stitches, cable 56; cat's eye 55; crossed insertion 53; cross-stitch cable 56; grand eyelet lace 54; loop 49; mock cable rib 56; moss 54; pattern 48-56; popcorn 55; purse 49; seed 54; twisted stockinette 52; woven basket 50; wrap 50
Stockinette stitch 20
Stocking hat 84
Straw 19
Stretching yarns 45
String 40, 47
Stuffed knitting 39, 63-64, 91
Suede 58; fake 97
Synthetics 19, 25, 40, 46, 87; blends 40, 42

Tassels 72
Testing yarns 45-47
Texture 36, 57
Three-dimensional knitting 32
Tools 17-19
Toys 39
T-pins 19, 45, 46
Tree shape 27
Triangles 23, 27, 28
Tubular crochet 94; knitting 33, 39, 63
Tweed effect 39
Twigs 31, 63
Twine 40
Twisted stockinette stitch 52
Two-color knitting 38

Varying textures 57
Vegetable dyes 57

Washability 61
Weaving in objects 31
Weaving seams 33
Wigs 64
Winding yarn 44
Wire 40, 74, 75
Wool 25, 34, 36, 42, 47
Woven basket stitch 50
Wrapping 75, 92
Wrap stitch 34, 50
Wristlet 100

Yarn needle 19, 80
Yarn over 20
Yarn winder 44